Narrow Gauge For Us

The Story of the
Toronto and Nipissing Railway

Narrow Gauge For Us

The Story of the
Toronto and Nipissing Railway

by Charles Cooper

THE BOSTON MILLS PRESS

The President & Directors of the Toronto & Nipissing Railway Company

request the Honor of Mr J. C. Bailey's Company

at the Opening of this Railway to Uxbridge

on Thursday, 14th of September.

Trains will leave Berkeley St Station, Toronto at nine o'clock Thursday Morning.
Please answer by the 9th inst.

Secretary.

Toronto, 1st September 1871.

This Card to be shown on entering the Cars,
and at the Town Hall Uxbridge.

Ontario Archives (Bailey Papers)

Canadian Cataloguing in Publication Data

Cooper, Charles, 1933-
  Narrow gauge for us : the Toronto & Nipissing
Railway

Bibliography: p,
ISBN 0-919822-72-X

1. Toronto & Nipissing Railway - History.
2. Railroads, Narrow gauge - Ontario - History.
I. Title.

HE2810.T67C66   385'.065'7135   C82-095156-0

Published in Canada by
THE BOSTON MILLS PRESS
98 Main St., Erin, Ontario NOB ITO

Typeset by Speed River Graphics, Guelph, Ontario
Printed by Ampersand, Guelph, Ontario

The Boston Mills Press gratefully acknowledges the assistance
of the Canada Council and the Ontario Arts Council.

 Winners of the
Heritage Canada
Communications Award

On the cover: Stouffville Junction at the turn of the century. *Hubert Brooks.*

603 ready to depart from Blackwater Junction for Midland in charge of Pacific-type 5062. 17 July 1958.
The Paterson-George Collection

Toronto & Nipissing Railway.

Managing Director's Office,

TORONTO, 4th December, 1872.

TO ALISON AND JONATHAN

To understand the past is to appreciate the present
and to catch a glimpse of the future.

Introduction

It is really rather difficult to imagine why anyone would have wanted to build a railway to Coboconk. But then, unlike in Europe, our early railroads were not built to transport people. A pioneer country needed lumber and grain to survive. This meant laying rails to wherever the timber was and as for the grain, much of the land was still unsettled and a railway line was a guaranteed attraction to encourage new farms.

To the capitalists and politicians of the day, the railway had no social significance. It was purely an instrument of economic development. Each was a risk venture designed to make money first and foremost, and more often than not, indirectly. The wholesaling of raw materials, the contracts for construction and the consequent real estate dealings were the real benefits. Most railways themselves did not actually make money as enterprises, or if they did, it was not for long and the employees and the ordinary users of the railway became pawns in a complicated and long drawn-out game of political chess.

In a country which could conceive of the Grand Trunk or the Great Western Railway, the Toronto and Nipissing might indeed have appeared as a jerkwater line, but that is a narrow view that does not take into account the reality of Ontario or that of transportation before the advent of the railway. With few roads and with those that existed either in a state of quagmire or dustbowl, depending on the season, movement on land was just as difficult, dirty and as dangerous, no matter whether the journey was to Goderich or to Uxbridge or wherever. It is just that depending on one's destination, the agony would last longer on some trips than others!

Ironically, it is the railway's local futuristic symbol, the CN Tower, which makes the point rather well. On a clear day from high up on the Observation Deck, one may view a sea of water and a sea of trees. Trees and trees and trees. Now in your mind's eye, take away all the buildings and the highways and just imagine nothing but trees, dense underbrush and torrential streams. Somewhere on the horizon to the north-east is the pioneering village of Markham and well beyond your gaze on even the clearest day is Uxbridge, let alone Coboconk. Now imagine saddling a horse and galloping off along some treacherous Indian trail thataway....

No doubt about it, for the ordinary citizen, the coming of the railway was a blessing of a lifetime. Admittedly a mixed one, in the view of some, but its benefits were undeniable. Until then, each community had lived its own life, substantially isolated and self-sufficient and every member of that community was completely inter-dependent on the goodwill and skills of his neighbour. At that time, travel to the next village was an adventure and a journey to the Queen City was a memorable event, and a picnic to Jackson's Point an ecstasy.

Yes, for many years, the local iron road was for most communities the only reliable link with the outside world. Thus, the railway was a boon. The men who worked on it were neighbours and the local depot a social institution, the focal point of the local economy and the nerve centre for the news of the world over the station agent's wire. The trains were as fibres woven into the tapestry of the life of the people, they took the children to high school, the farmers' wives to town for a day's shopping and they attended upon all other comings and goings. Young people left to seek their fortunes, soldiers went off to war, others came home to return to the place of their birth and together with those who just took the train for business or an outing, they all came under the friendly gaze of the engineer. In addition, the trains were the very lifeblood of the local economy in taking raw materials and produce to market in return for the finished goods to make life more bearable: implements for the farms, supplies for the school, gadgets for the kitchen and some finery for Sunday. The trains brought and took the mail and the mournful wail of the engine signalled breakfast, noon hour and quitting time. Life so regulated itself around "the daily" that even the cows would know without being bidden that it was milking time.

There were few improved roads and highways as we know them today, and it seemed as if life would always be that way.

You know the rest of it. Today the tracks are gone, the stations razed, the engines scrapped and the memories dimmed. Silence broods over the abandoned rights of way, with only the wind to whistle over the grass along the overgrown embankments.

So, briefly now, let us turn the pages and relive a bygone age the way it was. Smell the coal oil in the waiting room, hear once again the clattering milk cans, the creak of the station door, the excited chatter of bystanders, the sonorous whistle and the ringing bell of the engine, the impatient thump of the injectors and the conductor's loud and finite: "BOOOOARD!" Then feel the sudden lurch as the couplings clank and hear the coach groan as it takes the strain, press your nose against the soot-stained window and watch the place you called home grow smaller and disappear as the train rumbles across the trestle over the village creek and rounds the curve under a billow of smoke on its way to the big world out there around the hill....

CN 637 at Lindsay August 3, 1936. This engine, a workhorse Mogul from the Grand Trunk days was doing regular duty on the Lindsay-Coboconk run at that time. Jim Platt and The Paterson-George Collection

#5062 on the wye at Blackwater exchanging mail express cars with train 92. 17 July 1958. The Paterson-George Collection

CONTENTS

MAP INDEX

A double-header (Mikados 3228 and 3272) southbound at Blackwater Junction with 54 cars of stone from the Kirkfield Quarry. 8 August, 1958. The Paterson-George Collection

THE RIVALS

A pen and ink drawing of the first Toronto Union Station (1858-1871). The view is looking west. Of frame construction, it was situated just west of Bay Street. At first it served the GTR, GWR and NRC, but in 1866 the GWR pulled out and erected their own station just east of Yonge Street at the Esplanade on the site now occupied by the O'Keefe Centre. In 1868 the NRC followed suit, establishing their own terminal beside the St. Lawrence City Hall. Metro Toronto Library Board (JRR Collection)

Vision or Folly?

"Broad Gauge Principles, but Narrow Gauge for us." Thus proclaimed one of the banners at the opening of the Toronto and Nipissing Railway at Uxbridge. Not unexpectedly, our railway histories, if they mention this line at all, have given it a passing mention as a local colonization project. Fair enough. Compared to the Grand Trunk or the Great Western, the Toronto and Nipissing was definitely only a Fairlie among Moguls, but its appearance was not only of considerable significance to the Toronto of the day, but also was a rare, if not unique phenomenon, in its special characteristic of being the first operating public narrow gauge railway in North America.

First of all, it is important to look at the Toronto and Nipissing in the context of Toronto as a burgeoning city on the shore of Lake Ontario. It was an age of intense rivalry in all phases of Canadian society of the day, fanned to white hot fervour by all the customary Victorian virtues of thrift, industry and the respectability bestowed by the labour that conquered all. In a developing country such as the newly confederated Canada, each province, city, and village struggled to best its neighbour. Since the railway and the harbour were seen by the cities as the key to prosperity and since all local communities knew only too well that rails were imperative to survival, it should not be surprising that local citizenries eagerly poured staggering sums of money into the pockets of promoters for yet another road or to have the rails go through their burgh rather than their neighbour's town. In this dog-eat-dog competition Montreal was pitted against Toronto, Hamilton against Toronto, Whitby against Toronto, Port Hope against Whitby, Cobourg against Port Hope — each wanting *their* harbour to handle the lucrative wholesale trade arising from the trans-shipment necessary for onward movement to distant ports. This frenzied competition, with the railway as the driving force, had its origins in the proclamation of the steam locomotive as the force of the future at the Rainhill Trials in Lancashire, England in October 1829. No sooner had George Stephenson's "Rocket" been proclaimed the winner for a handsome prize of £500, than a fever of railway building broke out in Europe that was soon to be caught across the Atlantic Ocean. The charter for Canada's first steampowered railway, the Champlain and St. Lawrence Railroad was applied for in February 1832, to be followed by a rash of other applications, both in Lower and Upper Canada. Already, in June 1832, the Courier of Upper Canada finds itself advocating a rail connection to Lake Simcoe:

> "York is the natural inlet as well as outlet of general intercourse with
> Lower Canada.... Yonge Street is the natural line of communication....
> The bad state of the Yonge Street road for several months in the year,
> renders it almost impossible to pass to and from York with a loaded
> carriage.... A Rail Road from York to Lake Simcoe....will preserve to
> York and the Yonge Street road the natural advantages they
> possess...."

For many reasons, political, economic and geographic, the railway mania of Europe did not arrive in Canada until the 1850s but then Toronto had initiated its own first railway. Plans for this line had first been bruited as early as 1834 but nothing concrete happened until 1849 when the Toronto, Simcoe and Lake Huron Union Railroad was incorporated "to build from Toronto to Lake Huron and to Barrie etc." under the energies of one Frederick Chase Capreol, commission merchant, financier and an individual quite consumed by a lifelong passion for railways and an abiding belief in their future. The first train left for Machell's Corners (Aurora) on May 16, 1853 and unquestionably this event consolidated the commercial future of what 20 years previously was a struggling garrison town called Muddy York. This auspicious event was followed in quick succession by the opening of a

Toronto-Hamilton connection for the Great Western Railway in 1855 and again in 1856 the Grand Trunk Railway of Canada made its Toronto début with the arrival of its first train from Montreal in October, preceded by the opening of the Toronto and Guelph Railway (already a subsidiary of the GTR) in July of the same year. While at first glance this sudden influx of trackage should have secured the economic destiny of the fledgling city beyond all doubt, a moment's reflection will convey the sobering thought that neither the Great Western nor the Grand Trunk had Toronto's interests at heart, in the sense that their connections were designed to draw business away from Toronto rather than towards it.

Nevertheless, for the time being these railway connections were a step forward in establishing the city as a place of note. The two "comers-in" certainly added to municipal prestige and provided much-needed transportation links along the lake bord, but it was the little old Oats, Straw and Hay Railroad which had been revamped by the renowned F.W. Cumberland into the redoubtable Northern Railway of Canada that was bringing home the proverbial bacon — the timber, lumber, grain and other farm products that Toronto needed to sustain itself and turn a nickel on. As Toronto grew and its manufacturing base expanded, other interests wanted a share of the action and it was at this point that a number of different circumstances came together.

First of all, with the upturn in manufacturing and trade, the general economy had been reasonably buoyant since the early 1850s, providing the optimism and some much-needed capital to help finance this new-fangled invention. Then, with Confederation and the creation of Ontario and Toronto's reappointment as a capital city, a new patriotic spirit abounded and talk had already begun of a transcontinental railway. Even the most elementary knowledge of Canadian geography would enable anyone to appreciate that such a railway would pass somewhere through northern Ontario and then, unless all the western trade was to go to Montreal, those with Ontario's interests at heart had better start to think about tapping into this golden vein. At the moment, only the Northern Railway of Canada was even poised to make such a connection and competition was shaping up from Hamilton and Port Hope. Hamilton had derived considerable municipal benefit from the erection of the Great Western Railway shops in that city, but realized too late that the Great Western Railway did not benefit the city to any extent in bringing in raw materials and merchandise for the wholesale trade. While the Hamilton and Northwestern arrived on the scene too late to put a dent into the business being done by the Northern Railway of Canada, the proposed Wellington, Grey and Bruce Railway was a substantial threat to Toronto in diverting the prospective lucrative business from those lush counties, plus the trans-shipment traffic from the Lake Huron ports to Hamilton. Similarly in the east a competitive cloud, in the shape of the Port Hope, Lindsay and Beaverton Railway, was darkening the horizon. This railway had been chartered as early as 1846 in the name of the Peterborough and Port Hope Railway but lay dormant until 1854 when Port Hope decided that Lindsay and the lands beyond to Orillia and Georgian Bay were a better prospect. Port Hope may have decided to await the arrival of the Grand Trunk but the immediate success of the Ontario, Simcoe and Huron Union Railroad Co., as the Toronto, Simcoe and Lake Huron Railroad was renamed in 1850, was more likely to have been an overriding factor in the decision to change direction and to make a start. This railway arrived in Lindsay in 1857 and under its new name, The Midland Railway of Canada, continued westward and was opened for traffic to Beaverton by January 1, 1871 and by July 22, 1873, into Orillia. The threat was clear.

As if the thrust from Port Hope were not bad enough, more competition was looming from the port of Whitby. Admittedly it seems improbable today that the ports of Cobourg, Port Hope, Whitby or Hamilton could have seriously challenged Toronto's harbour, but that is a view borne from the benefit of knowing what happened. In fact, each of these places had its own plan to divert the Georgian Bay traffic from the sluggish Welland Canal and each had hopes of becoming the predominant market for the steadily increasing volume of produce of every kind from the many farms which had been nursed from woodland lots to prime agricultural concerns.

At any rate, Whitby saw itself gradually being sandwiched between the Port Hope and the Toronto interests. It had the pipe dream for some time of its own railway to Lake Huron

Shortly after the inauguration of the T&N, the second union station was opened (July 1, 1873) for use by the GTR and the TG&B. Note the dual gauge of the second track in from the water's edge. It was a magnificent edifice for its day and lasted until 1927 when it was replaced by the Union Station familiar to travellers today.
Metro Toronto Library Board

(the Port Whitby and Lake Huron Railway Company chartered in 1853) but when the word of the prospect of the Toronto and Nipissing got out, wishful thinking had to give way to resolute action, as the Whitby merchants all of a sudden saw their livelihoods draining away to Toronto. While the Port Whitby and Port Perry Railway was triggered by the prospect of the Toronto and Nipissing and not the other way around, these rivalries had a habit of feeding on each other and the promoters of both railways finished up in competition for the available funding (the Whitby, Port Perry charter was granted the same day as that for the Toronto and Nipissing and the Toronto, Grey and Bruce Railways). To make a long story short, the Toronto and Nipissing delegation simply overpowered the Whitby efforts. The turning point came at Uxbridge where it was a choice between a direct line to Toronto and a branch via Port Perry to Whitby. The result was a foregone conclusion, a crushing defeat for the Whitby crowd. Granted that the influence of Joseph Gould, patriarch of Uxbridge, was paramount in persuading the vote in favour of the Toronto and Nipissing Railway, the attraction of a direct line to Toronto was patently irresistible. Indeed, the Whitby and Port Perry Railway was built but it was too short and too late.

   With all these complex rivalries in progress on a larger scale, the immediate Toronto interests must not be overlooked.

   The Northern Railway of Canada was, as has been noted, strictly a Toronto enterprise. The Grand Trunk Railway's entry into Toronto was tolerated (except by George Brown), but everyone realized by now that in order to benefit from a railway, one had to be a terminal point or in a position to pull the financial strings and as far as the Grand Trunk was concerned, Toronto did not qualify in either category.

To date Toronto had only one railway to call its own and lucrative as it had been, its capacity had its limits. Not only that, the Northern Railway of Canada had been sponsored by the old-established families in Toronto, and was currently supported by such locally prominent figures as J.D. Ridout, Colonel G.T. Denison, The Hon. J.B. Robinson (President), F.W. Cumberland (Managing Director), G.P. Ridout, The Hon. G.W. Allan, R.L. Denison, The Hon. J.H. Cameron, R. Cassels and others.

As the pace of business intensified in the 1860s, newcomers began to make their influence felt and William Gooderham was part of this increasing influence. A native of Norfolk, England, William Gooderham (the elder) had engaged in the East Indian trade and served in the Imperial Army when he emigrated to Toronto in 1832 at the age of 42 "with 54 relatives and £3,000 capital," going into the milling business with his brother-in-law James G. Worts (and upon his death in 1834, taking his nephew, James G. Worts, Jr. into the firm). As his business became firmly established as part of the Toronto scene, he became a member of the Toronto Stock Exchange and the Board of Trade. He was a director of the Bank of Upper Canada, a founder of the Bank of Toronto; and his contemporaries were such notables as A.M. Smith (banker), William McMaster (wholesaler), Casimir Gzowski (civil engineer), W.P. Howland (politician, flour and grain dealer), Rice Lewis (hardware dealer) and many others. In his spare time he devoted himself to his church and good works such as encouraging the Mechanics' Institute. The Gooderham and Worts windmill was a Toronto waterfront landmark for many years. Their original distillery was begun in April 1858 and completed two years later. The building, an impressive edifice of Kingston limestone, still stands in the Gooderham and Worts compound, with several later buildings and the Mill Street tower, which was constructed in 1858. At its inception, this enterprise had a private switch from the Grand Trunk and a siding capable of holding 14 cars. At that time, the Grand Trunk Railway had recently (in 1857) connected its easterly Don Station and its westerly Queen's Wharf termini, but although the first Union Station was erected in 1858 by the GTR to serve itself and the Great Western and Northern Railways, the waterfront railway scene remained fragmented as the latter two railways split away and built their own stations to the east. This fragmentation was certainly an obstacle to the early development of Toronto as a freight transfer point, since only the Grand Trunk provided a through service in the literal sense. However, at that time, the real money was still to be made from the development of the hinterland. Although the distillery siding was quite satisfactory as the lifeline of the family business, what was really needed to further one's influence and to consolidate one's wealth, was one's very own railway line.

Not only that, the Grand Trunk was not the solid enterprise in the late 1860s as it came to be regarded in the 1890s and it was perhaps wise not to have all one's transportation eggs in the one railway basket. An alternative, no matter how modest, would have been a wise business decision and the recent failures of the Bank of Upper Canada and the Commercial Bank of Canada were eloquent reinforcement of this consideration.

All of these background influences and motivations came to a head with an urgent question of the day, namely the price of cordwood.

Toronto owed its progress to date to the success of the Northern Railway, but it was time to strengthen its trading influence and bring some competition to the affairs of the city. There has to be a catalyst for every new endeavour and while it is clear that the Gooderhams had the influence and resources to promote a new venture, it was one George Laidlaw, an ambitious young Scot, who made it happen. It was he who was inspired with a vision of railways as the key to progress and development and he possessed the rare combination of energy, political acumen, eloquence and the determination to make his vision come true. George Laidlaw was the quintessential salesman in identifying his prospect's needs and it was thus that he sold profits to the Gooderhams, development of the hinterland to the Government of Ontario, cheap cordwood to the people of Toronto and a ready outlet for their produce (and unwanted cordwood) to the farmers along the right of way.

Thus the stage was set in Toronto at about the same time as news began to filter through in the railway world of an innovative locomotive which was about to usher in a new dimension of an infant technology; to be proven out on a small privately owned railway in Wales.

The Doubleheaded Monster

Canadian railway history has tended to be somewhat unkind to the Toronto & Nipissing, even unkinder than to the Toronto, Grey & Bruce, probably because of its domination by William Gooderham Jr. and the consequent appearance of being a rich man's folly. In fact the T&N and its sister enterprise, the TG&B were carefully calculated instruments of expansion and were launched simultaneously. Their hallmark was their narrow-gauge and their ownership (one each) of a different kind of locomotive which came to be known as a "double-ended Fairlie."

In its timetables, the T&N liked to proclaim itself as "the first Narrow-Gauge Railway opened for traffic on the Continent of America." This was not exactly accurate unless one inserts the word "public" to distinguish the line as a common carrier. The Lingan Colliery Tramway in Cape Breton had started operations in 1861 with horsepower and had acquired a small tank locomotive in 1866. Also, the Glasgow and Cape Breton Coal and Railway Company opened for business in May 1871, whereas the T&N did not open for traffic until July 12, 1871 and then only as far as Uxbridge. The TG&B had reached Orangeville on April 17, and Mount Forest in November 1871; about a month after the T&N reached Cannington. Since the TG&B did not reach Owen Sound until June 12, 1873 with a Directors' Special and since the T&N was complete and open for traffic to Coboconk on November 26, 1872, it is true to say that the T&N was, as far as has been determined, the first public narrow-gauge railway to open for traffic on the Continent of North America, beating its sister railway (which had half as far to go again) by about six months and the Denver and Rio Grande Railway by only a hair's breadth and actually trailing slightly behind various other narrow-gauge railways in Central and South America.

The narrow-gauge concept was one of the most sophisticated promotions of all time in the global context of that day and age. For reasons of economy and geography, places such as Australia, Burma, The Cape Colony, Colorado, India, Luxembourg, Mexico, New Zealand, Norway, Portugal, Russia, Saxony, South America, Sweden and Wales embraced the narrow-gauge concept in adopting different gauges; ranging from 1'11½" to 3'7⁵/₁₆".

In doing so, special challenges had to be met and conquered in the design of locomotive power, with the result that it is really difficult to determine whether the engine came before the gauge or vice versa, although there were undoubtedly narrow-gauge applications on an experimental basis during the 1860s. Only some 40 years before, the idea of a smooth wheel gaining sufficient traction on a smooth surface such as a rail, to haul any kind of load, was so revolutionary that the notion of applying this principle to a miniature gauge seemed almost preposterous. At a time when the "normal" gauge widths ranged anywhere from the Stephenson gauge of 4'8½" and the exotic Brunel width of 7'0¼" with graceful locomotive designs of driving wheel diameters in the 6' to 7' range and relatively high centres of gravity, it was inevitable that someone somewhere should propose a low slung locomotive with multiple driving axles and heavy enough to hug the crudest of narrow gauge tracks and haul loads over mountain ranges simply beyond the capacity of the mainline breeds of locomotives.

The simple concept of doubling boiler capacity to gain additional drawbar strength whilst improving adhesion with the exceptional weight of such locomotives, was not altogether new. There had been three unsuccessful precursors of the double-boiler design, but it was one Robert Francis Fairlie (1831-85) who made the application a practical success. In 1864 he published a pamphlet entitled "Locomotive Engines" in which he expounded upon the shortcomings of conventional steam locomotives in favour of his articulated design with its superior steam generating capacity, adhesion, its ability to negotiate sharp curves and to do away with the necessity of turntables.

Robert Fairlie was born in Scotland of an engineering family and served apprentice-ships at Crewe and Swindon, the two foremost English locomotive depots of that day. He was then appointed as Engineer and General Manager of the Londonderry and Coleraine Railway in what is now Northern Ireland and then worked for a line in India before settling down in London, with the daughter of George England of the Hatcham Iron Works as his bride, and consulting contracts with railways under construction in South America and India.

At the same time as Robert Fairlie was forging his career, somewhat in the footsteps of Sir Charles Fox (1810-1874); civil engineer who designed the Watford Tunnel, built the first narrow-gauge line in India and acted as consultant to railway construction in Ireland, Denmark, France, Queensland and the Cape before being engaged by the T&N; the diminutive Festiniog Railway Company had the honour of influencing the course of events far beyond anything that Fate might have been expected to bestow on a hitherto obscure narrow-gauge railway in Wales.

The Festiniog Railway had opened as a slate carrying line in 1836, with a continuous downhill gradient, so that the loaded wagons could run down from the quarries to the coast, the horses which pulled the empties back up to the quarries getting a ride downhill in specially designed "dandy carts" popular with early incline railways that relied on horsepower. By 1850, heavier rails had been laid with a thought to the possibility of steam traction, but in those days 7'0¼" was all the rage in that part of the world and no one really could conceive of a practical steam engine for a diminutive gauge of 1'11½". By 1860 the traffic was such that the horses could no longer cope and Charles Spooner who had succeeded his father James as Chief Engineer of the road had to look around for steam traction. Tenders were called and a contract was arranged with Messrs. George England of the Hatcham Iron Works for two engines initially, which were to be delivered in 1863. (At

The "Little Wonder", the first patent double-boiler Fairlie locomotive ever built, shown here proving its worth at its trials in 1870 in the Welsh hills. This engine was built in 1869 at the Fairlie Engine and Steam Carriage Company and became the archetype of four decades of this locomotive design. **Festiniog Railway Company**

The "James Spooner", the first Fairlie engine supplied to the Festiniog Railway by the Avonside Engine Company in 1872. Its works number was 929-930, which dates it as being built sometime after the "Caledon" and the "Shedden". Festiniog Railway Company

that time a railway of less than a 4'8½" gauge was not allowed to carry passengers but in 1864 the Festiniog Railway applied to the Board of Trade to do so and was granted permission by Captain H.W. Tyler, then Chief Inspecting Officer of Railways, who, incidentally, was shortly afterwards in 1876 to resign this prestigious post to become one of the most powerful railway executives of the Victorian Era, namely the President of the Grand Trunk Railway Company.) Another two engines were added, but these still did not meet the demands placed on the line.

By now, Robert Fairlie had designed experimental double-ended articulated locomotives for the Neath and Brecon and the Anglesey Central Railways. By 1870, George England and Robert Fairlie were working on the development of Fairlie's Patent and the acquisition of the Hatcham Iron Works proved to be the catalyst of success. Under the name of the Fairlie Engine and Steam Carriage Company, the production of the "Little Wonder" for the Festiniog Railway was the vindication that had so far eluded Fairlie and the others who had gone before him. The "Little Wonder" was the first narrow-gauge application of the Fairlie Patent and it underwent most successful public demonstrations with visits by many eminent engineers from far and wide (including for instance an Imperial Commission from Russia) to the Festiniog Railway and rave notices in the technical press of the day. In fact it is a virtual certainty that the deputation to England by Messrs. Gordon, Shedden and Laidlaw in March 1870, as reported by the *Markham Economist*, included an inspection tour of the Festiniog Railway. It is evident that the paeans of praise for the narrow-gauge concept by George Laidlaw and others were spoken with all the evangelism of those who had seen the light for themselves.

With the success of the "Little Wonder," the Fairlie locomotive had proved itself to the world and there was a rash of orders from all over the globe and several locomotive works were busy filling orders for South America, Mexico and most of the other countries mentioned previously. There were at least nine British manufacturers of the Fairlie locomotive but of all the British companies, the Avonside Engine Company produced more Fairlies than any other builder between 1871 and 1881, including the five that are definitely known to have come to Canada. Three went to the Glasgow and Cape Breton Coal and Railway Company (Works Numbers 907/908, 909/910, 911/912) and the other two were probably shipped out together; one to the Toronto, Grey and Bruce ("Caledon" 862/863) and the other to the Toronto and Nipissing ("Shedden" 864/865).

The mighty "Shedden", the Fairlie Patent locomotive imported from the Avonside Engine Company, Bristol, England. This picture has appeared in various publications as dated 1879, ascribed either to Coboconk, or more likely, Scarboro Junction.

Left to right: John Bradley, conductor; Sid Vaughan, wood passer; Charlie Clark, engineer; William Lorimer, fireman; Samuel Merrifield, brakeman; John Gobbett, brakeman; Chine Long, brakeman. Boston Mills Press

While there were variations of the Fairlie Patent, both in use and never put into practice, the classic Fairlie is the double-boiler locomotive with two articulated power bogies (trucks), a central fire box and two smoke boxes and stacks. These were so totally different from the conventional locomotive design that they were labelled, understandably but somewhat unfairly, as freaks. There are many local references to this design, both complimentary and disparaging, but perhaps the most vivid is a contemporary description as a "two-headed fiery dragon, belching sparks and billows of black smoke from both her huge smoke stacks, as she raced or crawled through forests and farms of the backwoods country." Their main disadvantage was the limited amount of fuel and water they could carry but their principal asset was their low gravity and their articulation, which enabled them to negotiate sharp curves and gave them adhesive powers suited for tough gradients and rough road beds. They lacked stability at high speeds but they were not intended as express locomotives. The judgement of history seems to be that as a class, they were not altogether successful as a major form of locomotive power, except in Russia and Mexico, but this has to be tempered with the recognition that the Fairlies required careful maintenance and skillful operation. Certainly the T&N's "Shedden" seems to have been well regarded by its owners. For the technically minded, we are indebted to the research of the late Mr. Rowland A.S. Abbott, for the following data on the "Caledon" and "Shedden" sister locomotives:

Wheel Arrangement:	0-6-6-0
Cylinders:	11½" × 18" stroke
Wheels:	39" diameter
Bogie Wheel Base:	7' 6"
Total Wheel Base:	26' 3"
Boiler Barrels:	10' long, 3' 0³/₈" diameter
Tube Heating Surface:	858 sq. ft.
Water Tank:	1,400 gallons
Fuel Capacity:	200 cubic ft. wood

The Toronto and Nipissing took delivery of the "Shedden" at Toronto in the Spring of 1873, since the minutes of the Board Meeting held on April 2, 1873 record that the Collector of Customs was requesting $1,744.50 duty. (It is interesting to speculate what the T&N might have paid for the "Shedden." The "Little Wonder" apparently cost £1,950 and weighed around 20 tons. If double the weight had a rough relationship to the price, this would work out at around £4,000 or $20,000; at which rate the customs duty would be something just under 10%.)

Not too long after being taken into service, the Fairlie suffered a boiler explosion at Stouffville (of which more anon) and was apparently repaired, since her picture was taken at Scarboro Junction in 1879 and since she is referred to in the T&N Return to the Minister of Railways and Canals for 1880-81 as follows:

"The Fairleigh (sic) engine weighs 40 tons and her train is 20 cars and vans."

Her ultimate fate is not known for certain, but it is doubtful that it would have been economical or even technically feasible to regauge her upon amalgamation with the Midland Railway and it is most likely that she was scrapped when the 3'6" gauge was finally eliminated by 1883.

In all of the special interest for the Fairlie, it must not be overlooked that the T&N's roster otherwise consisted of the more conventional form of locomotive power and we are indebted to Mr. Omer Lavallée (Narrow Gauge Railways of Canada) for the table that he has reconstructed:

MOTIVE POWER

Number	Builder	Year	Type	Builder's No.	Name
1	Canadian	1871	4-4-0	83	—
2	Canadian	1871	4-4-0	84	—
3	Canadian	1871	4-4-0	85	—
4	Canadian	1871	4-4-0	86	—
5	Canadian	1871	4-4-0	87	—
6	Canadian	1871	4-4-0	88	Uxbridge
7	Avonside	1871	4-6-0	938	—
8	Avonside	1871	4-6-0	939	—
9	Avonside	1871	0-6-6-0	864/865	Shedden
10	Avonside	1872	4-6-0	932	—
11	Avonside	1872	4-6-0	933	—
12	Avonside	1872	4-6-0	934	—

Other locomotive names have been referred to by various sources as the Joseph Gould, the Gooderham and Worts, the William Gooderham Jr., the Toronto, the M.C. Cameron, the Brock, the Bexley and the Rice Lewis, but none of these has ever been confirmed or identified with any particular locomotive.

"Uxbridge", Toronto & Nipissing No. 6, fresh off the assembly line at the Kingston locomotive works. Notice the locomotive supported by a crude narrow-gauge track laid on top of the standard gauge. PAC C2604

It is clear though, that the Fairlie's reputation was made as a work horse on narrow-gauge railways. According to contemporary newspaper reports the "Shedden" was considered the pride of the line and the fact that the T&N evidently took the trouble to repair her in 1874 tends to bear this out. While the "Shedden" and indeed the narrow-gauge of the T&N may have been viewed locally as a curiosity, this was certainly not the case in a global context and, if anything, the T&N and her sister railway, the TG&B, are of special significance as far as Canadian railway history is concerned. Their construction was a necessity and, remarkable as it may seem today, the specifications conformed to the most up-to-date technology that was available in that day and age.

In conclusion, George Laidlaw championed the narrow-gauge concept to his dying day and wherever he went and whatever he wrote, he was fond of reciting the nine advantages of the narrow-gauge system and it is interesting to note that the "Fairlie system of locomotive" was enshrined as one of its main fatures:

1st. The large comparative saving in first construction.

2nd. The large proportion of paying load to non-paying or tare weight of train.

3rd. The great reduction of wear and tear of permanent way, through advantage gained by light rolling stock.

4th. Saving in reduced wear and tear of wheel tyres from reduced weight on each wheel.

5th. Large proportionate increased power of locomotives.

6th. Proportionate increased velocities gained by the light system.

7th. Greater economy in working traffic.

8th. Comparative increase in capabilities of traffic.

9th. Great advantage gained by the application of the Fairlie system of locomotive engines in concentrated power, equalization of adhesion of all the wheels to the rails, economy from reduced friction of wheel flanges, reduction of wear and tear to the permanent way, great saving in fuel, and economy in wages for given power secured.

FOOTNOTE

A locomotive and train in a simulated Toronto & Nipissing Railway livery with the locomotive bearing the number 269 was a commemorative train specially decked out for Huntsville Old Home Week in 1926 and other contemporary displays. This train had no connection with the Toronto & Nipissing Railway other than the name of the T&N which seems to have been picked at random as presumably having an appropriate pioneer type flavour. The locomotive was a GTR locomotive of GWR origin.

"The Cheapest Road to the Best Market"

Little is known of George Laidlaw in his youth, but he was born in Linassie, Scotland in 1828. His law studies at Edinburgh must have been too staid for him, for he ran away to sea and after many adventures, found himself taking part in the war between Mexico and the United States in 1848 and then joining the 49er gold rush. Despite finding enough dust to pay for a passage home to Scotland, his ambitions beckoned once more and he arrived in North America again in 1855. Landing in Toronto with $40, he obtained a position with Gooderham and Worts who set him to work at buying barley. He subsequently went into the grain wholesale trade for himself and began to do very well from his wharf at the foot of Church Street.

The potential of railways intrigued him as it did many of his contemporaries. That there was need for some new pipelines to stimulate local business, of that there was no doubt. What is remarkable is that George Laidlaw evidently realized the potential of narrow-gauge railways long before the success of the "Little Wonder," because he was already putting pen to paper in 1867 to extol the virtues of the narrow-gauge concept. These few years between 1867 and 1870 were crucial for Toronto's needs, as it turned out, in the context of an economy which shortly afterwards started to go downhill. It is for this foresight and his determination to risk everything on a concept which was substantially untried, that he deserves a place in Ontario history.

He set out to find out as much about the narrow-gauge concept as he could and then proceeded to bombard anyone who would listen with his oratory and his tracts:

"The Old Prince of the Railway Bonus Hunters" George Laidlaw — 1882, born Scotland 28 February 1828, died Coboconk 6 August 1889. **Mrs. Jean Shields**

"The writer has no knowledge of engineering, and in common with his co-adjutors, has no other objects to promote, save the advantage of the country, the prosperity of Toronto and their share of the great increase in business which will follow the construction of these necessary works."

His pamphlet was very convincingly put together for distribution among municipal bodies of farmers in which he set forth the advantages of doing business with Toronto. He would point out that for an acre of woodland to be put into agricultural production, the trees had to be cut down and destroyed at considerable cost, whereas there was an increasing market for lumber and cordwood at the end of the line which would turn a dead loss into a profit, all for the price of shipping it on the railway.

"What most retards the settlement of our wild lands, is the time and labour required to burn the timber, which is done at a cost of $14 per acre while, if railway facilities were afforded the settlers, they could sell it at remunerative prices."

Also, Laidlaw gave the public credit for knowing something of the inordinate extravagance which had attended railway construction during the 1850s and denounced unequivocally this excessive recklessness:

"We have had enough of political contracts, blundering, humbugging of municipalities, (Toronto is out about $2 million principal and interest) and money irretrievably sunk below the hope of dividends and the well known sequel — a few enriched and many fleeced."

In referring to the Grand Trunk Railway he said:

"Million after million have been tossed under various pretexts, into its voracious maw, and yet it continues hungry."

Then he would take his audience into his confidence and tell them that they had decided to build cheap, narrow gauge railways, with iron rails of 40 lbs to the yard, and cedar ties, which could be secured from forests along the proposed routes of railways, and that the construction cost was estimated at the modest figure of $15,000 per mile. The cost of maintenance and operation would be considerably less than was possible on the other lines, owing to the use of lighter rolling stock.

So was the campaign waged and eventually, after a stormy debate in the Legislature, the Act incorporating the Toronto and Nipissing Railway (31 Vic. Cap. 41) was passed on March 4, 1868, along with that for the Toronto, Grey and Bruce and the Whitby and Port Perry railways, among others. It is interesting to observe that both the Laidlaw railways had cordwood clauses:

"Shall at all times, receive and carry cordwood or any wood for fuel at a rate not to exceed for dry wood 2½¢ per mile per cord for all stations exceeding 50 miles, and 3¢ for all stations under 50 miles in full car loads, and for green wood 2½¢ per ton per mile.... Shall further at all times furnish every facility necessary for the free and unrestrained traffic in cordwood to a large extent as in the case of other freight carried over the said railway."

The battle had only just begun. With the Act passed, now came the mind-boggling job of raising the money and the back-breaking task of actually building the railway.

The details of the financial manoeuvrings are understandably tiresome to the reader but they were no less tiresome to those charged with making the railroad a reality. It is true that for a while George Laidlaw became a rich man, but it was at the expense of many bitter disappointments and the eventual breakdown of his health. Railway promoters were viewed with the same sort of distrust that land developers are seen today and indeed, the railway promoters were in fact the land developers of their day. Laidlaw, Worts and some of the other directors travelled extensively, addressing many audiences, explaining the benefits to be derived. Invariably, the slogan as coined by our indomitable Scot was "The Cheapest Road to the Best Market." The basic sales tool was of course the prospectus. The reception in various municipalities ranged from barrages of rotten eggs to polite applause and enthusiastic editorials. Markham, for instance, was a community that sniffed out the potential benefits of the railway and the bagmen had no difficulty in getting a handsome bonus and selling some stock besides. A local newspaper of the day, *The Markham Economist*, was friendly to the railway and has provided posterity with many snippets of news. Since an original prospectus has not surfaced, we are fortunate in that it was published verbatim and it is worth requoting for the insight as to the purpose of the road and the competition to be faced:

PROSPECTUS

The Provisional Directors of the Toronto and Nipissing Railroad, finding that further progress in the building of broad gauge railways in Canada, with English capital, was no longer financially practicable or expedient, for lines of railway projected for local traffic, and having become cognizant of the successful working for a number of years, of railways built on the 3' 6" gauge in the Kingdoms of Norway and Sweden, in the colonies of Queensland and New Zealand and also in India, and that these railways were capable of accommodating a traffic of about a million or a million and a half tons of goods per annum and of carrying passengers at a speed of 25 to 30 miles an hour, and seeing that the average speed of passenger trains, including stoppages, in Canada, does not exceed 20 miles an hour and that the local traffic on the Northern Railway (which offers a fair illustration of the traffic to be obtained on the Toronto and Nipissing Railroad) did not exceed 195,000 tons and 140,000 passengers, have therefore resolved to construct the Toronto and Nipissing Railroad on the 3' 6" gauge in the most economical and efficient manner consistent with a total cost of $15,000 a mile.

The Directors have also noted Captain Tyler's report on the Festiniog Railway, 2' gauge *(actual 1' 11½"—author)*, in Merionethshire, Wales, the freight and passenger traffic of which approximates closely to that of the Northern Railway, and with the exception of the lumber traffic, largely exceeds that carried on the Lindsay and Port Hope, or on the London and Port Stanley Railway.

With a view to a just apportionment of the risk incidental to capital invested in railway enterprise in Canada, it was also resolved to ask the municipalities most to be benefited by the construction of the railway, for one-third of the total cost of the railway, viz. $5,000 a mile by way of bonus or gift. This proportion of the cost has already been voted for the main line excepting less than $50,000 yet obtainable in debentures bearing 6%, payable in 20 years.

The Directors do not propose to extend the line beyond Coboconk towards Lake Nipissing unless subsidized by the Government of this province with land or money sufficient to guarantee the Company from the loss of any private capital to be invested in the section of the line beyond Coboconk. Nevertheless, the Company feel assured that the first section being successfully completed, the remaining sections will immediately receive aid from the Government to the extent necessary to secure construction of the line to the ultimate terminus at Lake Nipissing — thus ensuring to the proprietors of the first section the practically unlimited timber traffic as well as the general business of an immense new territory of 20,000 square miles.

The terminus of the first section being located on the Gull River, with access to all its tributaries, and to the Burnt River, ensures for this railway timber and lumber traffic to exceed in duration of supply and quantity the timber and lumber traffic of the Northern Railway, and which will undoubtedly exceed that of the Lindsay and Port Hope Railway, which amounted to nearly 100 million feet in the year 1868.

The sawn lumber traffic of the Northern Railway of Canada in 1868, amounted to only about 55 million feet, and the square timber traffic to 1 million, 600 thousand cubic feet."

Competition came from two quarters, namely the Port Whitby and Port Perry Railway and also from the Port Hope, Lindsay and Beaverton Railway. As previously mentioned, the battle with the Port Whitby and Port Perry Railway was won when Uxbridge voted for the Toronto and Nipissing road. As for the Port Hope, Lindsay and Beaverton Railway, the T&N had always wanted to be friends with them from the outset. To a letter appearing in the Lindsay *Leader*, suggesting that the T&N would hurt Lindsay, Laidlaw had this to say in his characteristic fashion:

"Nonsense! In 30 years there will be larger towns, 30, aye 60 miles further north than Lindsay. The Toronto and Nipissing Railway will create those towns. Lindsay meanwhile will prosper with the general prosperity of the surrounding townships. There is not an acre of land in north Ontario or Victoria, nor a bushel of grain, nor a saw-log, nor a horse or cow, sheep or lamb, neither pigs nor poultry, neither cord of wood, nor pack of wool, which would not be greatly increased in value by the competition engendered, and by the facilities afforded by a railway to this superior metropolitan market. Put your shoulders to the wheel, and very soon you will have markets at your doors for every article of farm produce and every stick in your woods. Reading and gossiping about the new railway won't build it. You must take active and decisive steps at once to encourage and assist the gentlemen who have taken the onerous task of constructing this line of railway.
'Suas è a Clann-Nan-Gael' (*Up with the children of the Gaels-Author*)"

And this eloquence was matched by another essay appearing elsewhere:

"The Toronto and Nipissing Railway was not projected to oppose the Port Hope and Lindsay Railroad, or rob either it or these towns of any of their well-earned business. The proposed route will pass about 15 miles north of Lindsay, the northern terminus of the Port Hope and Lindsay Railroad. The latter runs south-east, the former south-west, which renders competition along their route impossible.

But while we do not want to rob them of the handling of a board or a spar, we will have the share that the capital and the enterprise of this city may secure for itself of the produce of the interminable forests that stretch northwards, beyond the immediate vicinity of Lindsay 200 miles to Lake Nipissing."

The Toronto and Nipissing of course had a special incentive not to excite the citizens of Lindsay. In an amendment to their charter (32 Vic. Cap. 83) of January 23, 1869, "The said company shall have power to construct a branch of their railway from a point in the township of Brock to navigable water in the town of Lindsay." Not only that, another amendment (33 Vic. Cap. 42) later the same year "that in the event of the municipal authorities of the townships of Brock, Eldon, Bexley, Laxton, Digby, Longford and Somerville not handing over the debentures by February 1, 1870, the Company will have the power to construct a line from Uxbridge northwards via Lindsay to Lake Nipissing or to any intermediate point."

Raw power-play! It was a common ploy to use bonuses granted by municipalities furthest away from the starting point to help finance the first section and then to hope that the company could then borrow against the constructed portion to build the remainder. The further north the campaign for funds went, the trickier the canvass became. Brock Township proved to be a major stumbling block in first of all rejecting the T&N's assessment of $65,000 and the proposed by-law itself in favour of a revision which forced the railway to "expend a specific sum in making a road through this municipality." The good town fathers of Brock envisaged the prospects of lots of oompah as far as Uxbridge, with the construction of the next section left to a certain degree of chance! Eventually, the by-law was resubmitted to Brock for $58,000, was unexpectedly defeated and then when pared to $50,000, the T&N found itself in competition with promoters from the Port Whitby and Port Perry line who were campaigning for their branch to Uxbridge and an extension of their line to Beaverton. However, Brock finally did go with the T&N project — it had been touch and go (but not nip and tuck!) but the spectre of the Port Whitby and Port Perry road had finally been laid to rest.

Moreover, even though Laidlaw had disclaimed any competition between the T&N and the Port Hope and Lindsay Railroad, there was also a concerted move afoot to extend it to Beaverton with a successful campaign for a bonus of $40,000 from Port Hope and $50,000 from Thorah Township. All was not well in Laxton, Digby and Longford either, since the railway asked for $25,000 and eventually got $12,500. Even that was supposed to be with a promise that the line would terminate at Norland, but it was given orally and could not be enforced. No wonder then, that there was a stand-by route via Lindsay lined up!

Eventually, the financing fell into place with bonuses granted by the various municipalities as follows:

City of Toronto	$150,000	(the minimum necessary to have a Director on the Board)
Scarborough	$ 10,000	
Markham	$ 30,000	
Uxbridge	$ 50,000	
Scott	$ 10,000	
Brock	$ 50,000	
Eldon	$ 44,000	
Bexley	$ 15,000	
Somerville	$ 15,000	
Laxton, Digby and Longford	$ 12,500	
	$386,500	

Later on, Uxbridge threw in another $2,000 to secure the engine and car shops of the railway.

The balance of the financing was largely achieved from the sale of bonds, and an Ontario government grant of just over $100,000, calculated as $2,000 per mile to the Portage Road and $3,000 per mile beyond.

One of the difficulties of financing these ventures was persuading anyone to buy stock and this reluctance was natural. Everyone knew by now that the railways themselves lost money but that the indirect benefit to the community was incalculable. So the citizenry did not mind (up to a point) being taxed to pay for the road and if they wanted to make a personal investment, bonds were preferable to stocks because if the road defaulted, at least one stood a chance of getting interest payments from the successor company, whereas stockholders usually lost their investment and moreover, would not receive any dividends throughout those years that were "bad", and there invariably seemed to be more "bad" ones than "good" ones. So, as a rule, only enough stock was sold for the Directors to retain control and often the Directors would finance their stock purchases by discounting or taking commission on bond sales to themselves at the expense of the other subscribers. While such practices would surely be considered improper by today's fiduciary standards, they were accepted as being within the bounds of Victorian honesty and there was at least no discernible outright dishonesty on the T&N Railway as opposed to the Port Whitby and Port Perry which had terrible problems with milked contracts. In fact, the competition could have had the jump on the T&N if they had played a straight game. The T&N did have problems getting their financing together but once the surveys were done and the contract was let to Ginty the construction went smoothly, with all the various obligations being performed with energy and integrity. And in all of this, Laidlaw himself ran a sterling financing campaign — smooth, eloquent, hard-hitting and professional. No wonder that he was dubbed "the Prince of the Bonus Hunters."

In the meantime of course there had to be a sod turning ceremony. As a matter of fact, both the Laidlaw railways had their ceremony within a few days of each other, the T&N ceremony taking place in Cannington on Saturday, October 16, 1869 with the first Premier of Ontario, The Hon. John Sandfield Macdonald, officiating, assisted by the President of the road, R.W. Elliott. The spade used at the ceremony has been preserved at the Victoria Museum in Lindsay.

It is interesting to speculate why the sod turning ceremony was held at Cannington, when the parallel occasion for the Toronto, Grey and Bruce took place at Weston. One might have supposed that Scarboro Junction or even Uxbridge would have been logical locations from a geographic point of view. Could it have been the difficulties with the Brock Township bonus? Or the fact that the sale of shares was moving at an abysmal snail's pace? Whatever the reason, someone had obviously reasoned that there was little point in preaching to the converted and that a little pomp and glitter would help to spread the gospel in a part of the country that had come to view these various promotions with a good deal of skepticism.

The Cannington ceremony was a directors' party and as was general for railway companies in particular, the roster of directors was constantly changing, but in 1869, the *Markham Economist* reported it as follows:

> President — John Crawford, M.P.,
> Vice-President — J.E. Smith, Esq., Collector of Customs
> Directors:
> Hon. M.C. Cameron, Provincial Secretary; Hon. D. Reesor, Senator; W.F. McMaster; Captain Taylor; William Gooderham, Jr.; H.S. Howland; George Laidlaw; H.P. Crosby, M.P.P.; Joseph Gould; Thomas Wilson; John Gordon (President of the TG&B); A.M. Smith; T.C. Chisholm; D. McRae, Reeve, Eldon Township; Edward Wheler; John Leys; R.W. Elliott; Alderman F.H. Metcalf; A.P. Cockburn, M.P.P.; J.C. Fitch; Alderman Dickey; James E. Ellis; John Shedden; J.D. Merrick; Dr. Wright.

Unfortunately, the early minute books from 1868 to 1873 have not been preserved, but it appears that John Crawford was the first President of the enterprise, to be succeeded in 1869 by R.W. Elliott (later associated with Laidlaw's Credit Valley Railway).

Commemorative turning of the sod ceremony, Toronto & Nipissing Railway at Cannington, 16 October, 1869.

Directors' Party, left to right: Edmund Wragge (Chief Engineer), J.E. Fitch, George Laidlaw, Joseph Gould, The Hon J.B. Robinson, R.W. Elliott (President), Sir John Sandfield Macdonald, Prime Minister of Ontario officiating, J.E. Smith, J.C. Leys, the Hon G.W. Allan, Mayor S.C. Harman, W.F. McMaster, H. Brethour, James Graham.

The spade used at this ceremony has been preserved at the Victoria Museum, Lindsay; donated by Premier Leslie Frost. Ontario Archives

By the time of the sod turning the whole of the line had been under survey for several months, including a visit from Sir Charles Fox, the consulting engineer, who "is very much pleased with Markham and Scarborough and says the country here very much resembles England. He also stated that the road will be more easily built than he anticipated, and at less cost."

The route of the line from Markham to Uxbridge was settled by July 1869 but the original proposal called for the Unionville Station to be on Hagerman's Hill, which did not go down too well in Unionville. The *Markham Economist*, with Markham's Station secure, smugly advised their neighbours not to be too picky about the choice of route:

> "We hope therefore that our friends to the west will not ask too much,
> as the means of the Company are limited and all should desire its
> success without pressing on it conditions that cannot be carried out."

This might be freely translated as "Pull up the ladder, Jack, we're all right." Anyway, the outcome was that Unionville's squire, H.P. Crosby, M.P.P. and the owner of the Union Mills wielded some influence with his fellow directors, with the predictable result that the line was plotted through Unionville along the route that it takes today.

In September 1869, our contemporary commentator reported that "The Company has entered into a provisional agreement with the Grand Trunk Railway to lay down a third rail, for its exclusive use, on the track of that Company along the wharf frontage, so that the Toronto and Nipissing Railroad will be able to deliver freight direct to any or all of the elevators. Altogether very fair progress has been made."

By March, 1870, R.W. Elliott stepped down as President and John Shedden was elected in his place, his first duty being to travel with John Gordon (President of the Toronto, Grey and Bruce Railway) and George Laidlaw to England to arrange for the purchase of rails and locomotives. It was undoubtedly on the occasion of this trip that they could not have failed to witness the "Little Wonder" hauling its prodigious loads on the Festiniog Railway. Meantime, back home, the *Markham Economist* noted that two engines and thirty flat cars were busily engaged in ballasting the road for 15 miles north of Scarborough, with stations already built at Scarborough, Agincourt, Unionville and Markham.

Passenger cars were to be 35 feet long, capable of accommodating 40 passengers each, platform (flat) cars, 30 feet long and box cars 15 feet long (it is clear that these had to be four-wheelers!). This is corroborated by a further report in the *Markham Economist* of December 8, 1870 that "Several freight and passenger cars are now lying in the workshops of Messrs. William Hamilton & Son of Toronto ready for use. The passenger cars are 35 feet in length, 10½ feet broad, only 1 foot narrower than the ordinary broad gauge. Each car has 18 seats, 9 on each side (36 passengers per car?), cane bottoms, cane backs with iron arms and are as comfortable as cushioned seats and will be much freer of dust *(not to mention cheaper—Author)*. Each car has an elevated roof with 4 ventilating windows (i.e. of clerestory design). They are plainly but tastefully ornamented, and the outside is painted a straw colour and looks very much like the cars of the Northern Railway of Canada." Also the Trouts in their "Railways of Canada" mentioned that "The locomotives are made by the Canadian Engine and Machinery Company at Kingston, a Fairlie engine of 42 tons weight and another large freight engine are being made in England."

At the time that J.M. and Edward Trout produced their compendium "The Railways of Canada" in 1871, the line itself had been finished to Uxbridge. Here Messrs. John Ginty and Company, who had the contract for the earthwork, let go in favour of Mr. Duncan McRae, M.P.P. on the same terms. One authority (G.R. Stevens) has suggested that Ginty could no longer stand the Gooderham directives, but McRae wielded a lot of influence in Eldon and it seems equally probable that there was a little back-scratching going on with the Eldon bonus, since the worst of the excavation was over at Uxbridge and any earthworks contractor with an eye to business, no matter how demanding the customer, would want to make up his money in the flat lands. Other contracts went to Edward Wheler of Stouffville for the fencing and ties to Uxbridge, and for the tanks and engine houses north of Uxbridge, and to Messrs. Wardrop and Co. for the track laying.

"The Toronto and Nipissing Railway Company have put on their line a splendid composite car of three compartments — a smoking room, post office and baggage room. The car is elegantly furnished, economically built, and a boon to smoking travellers." The Markham Economist, *28 March 1872* **Boston Mills Press**

Readers of local railway lore have come to accept with resignation the various dates that are usually offered with regard to the first train over any given line. Depending on whether the date refers to an inspection train, first passenger train, ballast train or the grand opening itself, not to mention the date that the railway *planned* to open, one is likely to have one of several dates to choose from. The *Markham Economist* of May 25, 1871 advised that "The first passenger car passed over the Toronto and Nipissing Railroad between Toronto and Uxbridge on Tuesday, 23rd last. Among the passengers were Messrs. Brydges, Grand Trunk Manager, Laidlaw, Chisholm, Gould, Stephenson, Elliott, Shedden, Wheler, Wragge, Crosby, Jones and others."

A further report says that "the ballasting is complete to Markham, being done up to Uxbridge. Crossings will follow trying to get ready for July 1st." It should be noted that the pioneering approach to ballasting was to get the track laid and then to dump gravel between the ties, not to lay the track on a bed of gravel!

Apparently the line was not quite ready as planned but opened without special fanfare on July 12, being followed by a visit from a Mr. Carl Pihl, who had engineered the narrow gauge construction of Norwegian Railways.

On September 14, 1871, came the grand opening bash: "At all the stations, beautiful arches were strung across the track and the reception route elegantly festooned."

According to the a local diary kept by one Elizabeth Christie, "At length about 1:00 o'clock the whistle sounded with the cry 'Here they come' and the Rice Lewis and the Joseph Gould came shrieking along over fire crackers with 6 or 7 cars from which issued a stream of gentlemen and the band of the 10th Royals. I at once recognized M.C. Cameron's thin form and face and cold searching eye looking around for old acquaintances."

The ceremonial opening of the T&N, an historic sketch from the Canadian Illustrated News of October 7, 1871. The view is along Brock Street towards town. The floral arch is at the crest of Brock Street to the right of the picture and the large decorated building is the news storehouse of Horsman and Kelly. To the left of that building is the water tower, enginehouse and behind and to the left of the enginehouse, the first station building.
Metro Toronto Library Board

The Uxbridge station was elaborately decorated with an arch of evergreens and the motto on the building was "Onward to Fort Garry." Other banners were "Space Conquered," "Labor omnia vincit" and (significantly) "The Old Times have Vanished" and others, among them, "Broad Gauge Principles, but Narrow Gauge For Us."

In the evening, there was the banquet and an elaborate succession of toasts which had been designed to ensure that all the political axles remained properly greased, including one to the "Railway Interests of Canada" which concludes as follows:

> "However much some persons may feel against the GTR, that institution has dealt with the narrow gauge railways in a most liberal spirit, and without the hearty cooperation of the directors of that road, the new lines of railway would not be in so prosperous a condition as they were at the present time."

This is, without doubt, a reference to the Grand Trunk Railway cooperation in allowing both the TG&B and the T&N to lay third rails on the Grand Trunk right of way to gain access to the waterfront, without which neither enterprise would have served the purpose that their promoters had intended.

With the festivities over, the road now had to get down to earning its keep. At the end of October, 1871 the line reached Cannington and "In the course of the present month, it is expected trains will be able to make connections with the Beaverton and Lindsay Railway" (November 18, 1871).

Apparently a dinner was held on a Toronto and Nipissing train in December 1871 to which directors from the Midland Railway were invited "For the purpose of endeavouring to make friendly running arrangements with them and with the hope that the connection would compete with the Northern Railway."

A timetable duly appeared in the local papers advertising trains as follows:

	A.M.	P.M.	A.M.	P.M.	Single Fare
Berkeley Street (Toronto)	7.45	3.30	10.45	6.40	
Scarboro Junction	8.20	4.10	10.10	6.10	.35
Agincourt	8.37	4.30	9.45	5.45	.55
Unionville	8.57	4.50	9.20	5.20	.65
Markham	9.10	5.05	9.10	5.05	.75
Stouffville	9.40	5.40	8.45	4.40	.95
Goodwood	10.05	6.10	8.20	4.15	1.10
Uxbridge	10.35	6.40	7.45	3.45	1.30
Wick	11.10	7.15	7.10	3.10	1.55
Sunderland	11.30	7.35	6.40	2.50	1.65
Cannington	11.55	8.00	6.25	2.25	1.85
Woodville	12.15	8.20	6.05	2.08	1.95
Midland Junction	12.25	—	—	2.00	1.95

(Author's Note — The fares were not included as part of the timetable. They were obtained from another source and have been appended for ease of reference.)

This was as of January 1872. A later timetable, once the line had been extended to Coboconk (completed and opened for traffic November 26, 1872) shows that the time of the morning mail train from Toronto had been improved by 45 minutes to Midland Junction (but still terminated there) and the afternoon express train now left Toronto at 4.05, with a 42 minute improvement to Woodville and arriving at Coboconk at 10.10 p.m. (The single fare all the way to Coboconk was $2.75. Considering that a labourer's wage was a dollar a day, these fares were not cheap.) Interspersed between the two was a mixed train from Uxbridge to Coboconk and return which of course was very slow. In the midst of all this, the usual operating headaches and problems of living up to all the promises were not long in coming. Although at the outset the T&N shipped more cordwood than any other commodity, complaints were rife at Agincourt, Markham and Goodwood:

> "It was sometimes hard to get large and influential companies to act up to agreements. Someone had said that 'Companies had no souls to be damned nor posteriors to be kicked.' They could generally manage to evade drawing cordwood on the grounds of not having the rolling stock to spare, etc."

There was a prompt reply from the railway, advising of improvements that were being made and the minutes record additional purchases of flat cars:

> "Notice is hereby given that, on and after January 8, 1872, the Company will be prepared to carry cordwood, as well as other freight, from all stations along the line to Toronto; and, in order to afford every facility for this traffic, arrangements are being made to give increased accommodations at the various stations for piling.

As this is the proper season for cutting and hauling cordwood, parties requiring accommodation are requested to see the Station Masters, and arrange for the necessary space to pile their wood. The Directors expect that this road will be in running order to Coboconk in August next; and as additions are being made daily to the rolling stock, every reasonable facility will be afforded for sending forward with despatch all cordwood, lumber, timber, grain, etc., that be offered for carriage."

Despite all of this, the problem gradually got worse. By 1874 farmers all along the line were complaining that there were never enough cars to take the cordwood to market and that they were being forced to sell it to the railway at the railway's price in order to get rid of it. The householders in Toronto were angry too because the price of cordwood was going up (and this in a depression yet) and there was finally such a public outcry that the price did drop, but farmers were still holding meetings to see what could be done to stop the railway from monopolizing the firewood trade. While it is convenient to accuse the railway of sheer greed (which was undoubtedly a factor considering that the railway naturally sought to compensate in a period of inflation for the fixed transportation rates permitted by their charter), the other part of the problem was the limited capacity of the line to cope with the flood of traffic that besieged it.

After all, the line had been designed for this very purpose and it was strictly a plan that had succeeded only too well. The lumber and cordwood being shipped from the northern end of the line simply left no room for consignment "from the lower end," combined undoubtedly with the fact that the railway would make a little more with a longer haul than a shorter one. The essential difference in railroading between Europe and North America has always been the overwhelming volume of freight traffic, but in 1870 this was difficult to envisage. The same problem was developing on the Toronto, Grey and Bruce Railway and the handwriting was starting to shape itself on the wall for the narrow gauge concept.

The Branch

The relationship of the Sutton Branch to its Toronto and Nipissing parent was intended to be one of mutual benefit. The communities along what is now Highway 48 between Ballantrae and Sutton naturally wished to take advantage of an opportunity to make a convenient connection with Toronto, and the Toronto and Nipissing visualized a captive feeder line with a wharf on Lake Simcoe at its most northerly point. As a bargain went, both got more or less what they expected but it was an arm's length and even an acrimonious relationship.

As early as March 1872, a preliminary discussion was held between representatives for the branch line and the Toronto and Nipissing. The townships involved were to contribute $100,000 in bonuses, with the hope of the usual government grant of $2,000 a mile, which would net something just over $50,000. The principal mover and shaker here was Robert McCormack, born in 1818 in New York State of United Empire Loyalist stock. He established himself as a millwright and in 1852 became a lumber man in the north-easterly section of Whitchurch. He, along with a number of other local businessmen and landowners, including J.R. Stephenson, J.N. Blake, J.R. Bourchier, John Ramsden, R.A. Riddell, Donald MacDonald, William H. Summerfeldt, Angus Ego, Robert Rowland and David Baker formed the provisional directorship of the Lake Simcoe Junction Railway who elected A.G.P. Dodge, M.P. to be President and Robert McCormack to be Vice-President of the Company, on May 1, 1873 at the offices of the Company at 56 Church Street in Toronto. The charter had been approved on March 29, 1873 (36 Vic. Cap. 75), thanks to the intercession of William F. McMaster (merchant and Director of the Toronto and Nipissing Railway) with full power to lay track, construct piers, wharves, etc. on Lake Simcoe; to construct, purchase, charter and navigate boats or vessels on Lake Simcoe "and the waters adjacent thereto"; to enter into a leasing agreement and to take out gravel for ballasting. The charter required the road to be completed in five years and it also had a 3¢ cordwood clause.

The Government of Ontario duly came across with $53,000 and the townships contributed as follows, for once without recriminations or revocations — everybody wanted the railway:

The County of York, comprising Georgina, North Gwillimbury and the easterly six concessions of East Gwillimbury Township	$45,000
North Gwillimbury Township	$20,000
Georgina Township	$20,000
Whitchurch Township	$15,000
	$100,000

Conspicuous by its absence is a contribution from Toronto. By this time the financial panic of 1873 had occurred and the meeting of June 3, 1875 noted dolefully that the by-law, "was not submitted for want of sufficient support on the part of leading citizens and by reasons of the large expenditures which would, under the circumstances, have to be made to order to secure a chance of success." However, at the same original company meeting of May 1, 1873, the directors authorized the President and Managing Director to negotiate with, among other things, the Toronto and Nipissing Railway Company for a lease in return for

25% of the gross receipts and to have the Toronto and Nipissing guarantee the bonds to the extent of $150,000 (approximately 25% of the total issue), to exchange free passes and to carry freight at the same rates as the T&N over T&N tracks.

This turned out to be a protracted affair. In a letter to Mr. J.C. Bailey, the chief engineer of the Lake Simcoe Junction Railway, Mr. C.G. Hanning, the Uxbridge surveyor who was being hired by both companies for their respective needs, said:

> "I am in receipt of yours of the 16th inst. (16 November, 1875) instructing me to proceed with a survey of the extension of the T&N railway to Norland.... I am now engaged in getting up plans of the right of way for the Lake Simcoe Junction which will be finished I hope early next week...."

So the survey was not done until the end of 1875, while the contractor (Mr. F. Shanly) was not appointed until the meeting of June 1, 1876. By this time, the Company had moved its headquarters to 10 Adelaide Street East. At the same meeting, the shareholders voted to pay Mr. Blake for his services in bonds of the Company, about which he wasn't too happy. Inexplicably, Mr. Bourchier of Sutton resigned as a director on July 7, 1876, possibly in protest against the appointment of Naismith & Company as contractors, or the appointment of Mr. Bailey as chief engineer or the appointment of Mr. Kingsford as solicitor, or Mr. Blake's improved basis of remuneration, all of which occurred the next day.

The agreement with the Toronto and Nipissing Railway was not actually ratified until October 19, 1876 (for a 21 year lease) and even then there were a few little niggles still being ironed out here and there: "That neither the Company nor the contractors are bound to furnish any more land at Stouffville than is required for right of way, siding accommodation to the length of half a mile and land for a turntable and engine house and approaches thereto, in accordance with the terms of the agreement with the T&N railway company and the contractors and that the chief engineer be instructed to lay out the road."

And again:

> "That the Chief Engineer be instructed to lay out the dock at Jackson's Point in such a way that any steamer or other large vessel can come up along the south side of the old dock and make use of same. That the docks be built on piles, according to the terms of the agreement with the Toronto and Nipissing Railway Company and the contract with Naismith and Company and that this Company considers that under such contract and agreement, a portion of the dock should be built in sufficiently deep water to allow the largest steamer on the lake being moored alongside. That this company is not bound under the terms of the agreement with the Toronto and Nipissing Company, nor do they consider the contractors are bound, to furnish more than the ordinary right of way and siding of half a mile in length at Jackson's Point and that the old dock and warehouse are not required by the company and need not be purchased by the contractors."

In the meantime, the Lake Simcoe Junction Railway had an amendment to their charter put through on February 10, 1876 (39 Vic. Cap. 76) which, among other things, gave them the power "to extend to some point on the line of the Port Whitby and Port Perry Railway or to any port on the shore of Lake Ontario within the said county." There is no record that this was ever surveyed. It certainly did not make economic sense and from an engineering point of view, the line would have had to swing straight due east through Claremont to Myrtle, or from Brougham to Brooklin or directly to Whitby, either of which routes would have called for a substantial amount of excavation and grading. Obviously this amendment was made for the sole purpose of giving the Lake Simcoe Junction Railway some leverage with the Toronto and Nipissing.

With all the bickering just about done, the line was built and open for traffic on October 1, 1877.

The following are interesting engineering sidelights. On December 4, 1877, a letter from Mr. D. McKenzie, resident engineer of the Lake Simcoe Junction Railway to Mr. Bailey, his boss:

"Messrs. Naismith and Newman are at work doing the things called for in the report. I think they will be able to finish them this week. The following is the amount of sidings built:

Stouffville	2,049'
Ballantrae	610'
Vivian	1,271'
Mount Albert	1,272'
Ravenshoe	1,166'
Sutton	2,076'
	8,444'

This leaves 2,116' of siding to make up the 2 miles required by contract. The position of the frog at Jackson's Point will give a length of 850' of siding at that place when it is completed to the outside of the wharf, which will leave 1,266' to be used as you may see fit. I think that the length of 850' at Jackson's Point will give ample siding room for years to come. I understand that Mr. Gooderham has promised a siding at Zephyr sideroad. If this be the case, some of this iron could be used there. If you require a greater length of siding at Jackson's Point, please let me know before Newman gets through so he can lengthen it."

Another report notes that there is to be a water tank, water closet, engine house and turntable at Sutton; a water closet at Blake Station (Ravenshoe/Brown Hill); a water tank and a water closet at Mount Albert, a water closet at Vivian and an engine house and a turntable at Stouffville. It seems likely that the water closets were for use with the Haggas Water Elevator, more of which anon. Another report in the Shanly Papers (reference MU2689A24d Box 26) provides other engineering specifications, including those for the stations. The station houses at Sutton and Mount Albert were to be equal to Stouffville; the station house at Blake/Ravenshoe/Brown Hill was to be equal to Kirkfield, Vivian was to be similar to Eldon, Ballantrae similar to Milliken, the engine houses at Stouffville and Sutton were to have two stalls, the tanks and tank houses at Sutton and Mount Albert were to be similar to those at Cannington and the turntables at Sutton and Stouffville were to be the T&N standard pattern. The dock at Jackson's Point was to be built on piles and to be large enough to hold four 8-wheeled freight cars.

Thus did the Lake Simcoe Junction Railway come into being, but like many other railways of its day, it entered the game too late to establish itself and prove its worth as a local enterprise. It certainly contributed its share of revenue to the T&N, but although it produced as much as it could be expected to, from the point of view of the T&N it was too little and too late to stave off the inevitable.

For many years a mystery, this fine post card has been identified as being a picture by A&D Grant, a professional Sutton photography firm of the early years. This is the grand opening in 1877 of the LSJR with the "Uxbridge" of the T&N doing the honours. This is not incongruous, since the LSJR was to be operated under the lease with T&N equipment. Hubert Brooks

Masters and Servants

For many years, railroading was a primary occupation in Canada and there are few families established here since the mid-19th century who cannot include at least one railroader in their midst. In the early days, a combined 40 or 50 years' service with various railroads was not uncommon and an exceptional railroading family such as the Heels are well known in Midland and Lindsay, with a record of a combined total of over 800 years of railway service. It was in the mid-1800s that many young men who had apprenticed with some railway in England sought work in Canada and many others went into this line of work simply because it was available.

This account appeared in the *Toronto Telegram* in 1922 as an interview with an old-timer by the name of John Duncan who started by helping his father at the old Thornhill (Concord) Station on the Northern Railway of Canada in 1855 and who was eventually to become General Superintendent of the Toronto and Nipissing. He recorded this reminiscence in his eightieth year:

"I started work with the old Toronto & Nipissing in 1873 about a year after it was built. It was one of the two narrow-gauge lines out of the city and ran to Coboconk via Markham and Stouffville, and later had a branch to Jackson's Point. The tracks were only 3'6" wide. The first engine, the "Gooderham & Worts" only weighed about 25 tons, and the cars were about 40 to 45 feet long, and, though necessarily narrow, had accommodation for about 60 people. They made pretty good time, too — up to 35 and 40 miles an hour. The late Mr. William Gooderham, uncle of the present elder generation of that family, was Managing Director of the road, and more than once when he was travelling, I have heard him send instructions to the engineer not to run so fast, as it would wear out the light 40-pound-to-the-yard rails. We sometimes ran excursions, principally to bring country folk into town. We often used freight cars for the purpose, but people weren't particular about accommodation in those days. We called these summer trips "watermelon excursions," as most of the travellers provided themselves with big melons for refreshment. The farmers would even get up on top of the cars, and this dangerous practice worried Mr. Gooderham very much, but it was hard to regulate the farmers. A famous double-header locomotive hauled many thousands of tons of freight between Toronto and Lorneville Junction on the T&N. This engine, on which Charles Clark, now living on Spadina Avenue, was once a fireman, blew up at Stouffville, in the late 70s *(sic)* and killed everyone near it. Chief freight on the Toronto & Nipissing was, of course, lumber and cordwood. Vast quantities of the latter, cut on innumerable farmers' bush lots, came into Toronto, being disposed of to various dealers through the Gooderham interests, which controlled the railway. Among the early cordwood dealers was Robert John Fleming, destined later to become Mayor of Toronto, and later still, General Manager of the Toronto Railway Company. The Toronto & Nipissing went out of business as such, in 1882, when it was sold to the Grand Trunk for $1,400,000 and converted into the standard gauge line which today serves the territory."

The attraction of railway work was that it was steady employment for wages that compared favourably with other jobs on the farms or in the sprouting factories. It was a fresh air job spiced with danger and glamour and offering a camaraderie that could only be equalled in uniform. True the life was arduous and constantly took one away from home, at least in the "running trades," but if one stuck it out and learnt on the job, one could get to be a conductor, engineer or station agent, or perhaps yardmaster or roadmaster. All of these jobs, especially those of conductor and station agent, held considerable prestige in Victorian society. In fact the station agent in a small community held a position quite at par with the local preacher, teacher and reeve.

As soon as it became known that a new railway was to be built, men from other railroads would flock to it in the hope of promotion and newly arrived immigrants saw it as a chance to get a start. The terms of employment were essentially no different on the railways than in any other line of endeavour in the mid-Victorian economy. Labour was plentiful and cheap and labour unions were unheard of, so that employers were quite free to set their terms. By and large this was to obtain as much as possible for as little as they could get away with, salving their consciences with sprinkled acts of patronage so that their labour force would have an opportunity to revere and elevate them to local sainthood.

The firm of Gooderham and Worts clearly did not set out to be in the railroad business; they became railroad employers so that their real business of distilling and the wholesale of grain could survive and prosper. A contemporary account (1880) of their business enterprise records it as "a firm of considerable commercial importance," devouring in one season 500,000 bushels of Indian corn imported from the western United States, 100,000 bushels of rye and 10 tons of hops from the Bay of Quinte, 50,000 bushels of barley and 25,000 of oats from around Toronto. Obviously the firm were good customers of the Grand Trunk Railway but the contribution of the T&N was not to be overlooked.

The Railway Return for the same year (1880) shows that the T&N carried 523,878 bushels of grain, 378 carloads of live stock, close to 10,000,000 feet of lumber and 33, 814 cords of firewood (in the days when a cord was 128 cubic feet), as well as 7,532 tons of manufactured goods, over 40,000 barrels of flour, 6,036 cans of milk, 58,339 bushels of potatoes, 30,139 barrels of salt, lime and plaster, and 230 cars of stone and coal, for a total tonnage of 120,500, with a total revenue of slightly in excess of $1 per ton carried. The need of the distillery itself was only about 15% of the grain carried and the rest was destined for the wholesale trade. The firm was founded as a milling business in 1832 when William Gooderham, Sr. formed a partnership with his brother-in-law, James G. Worts. The firm was then known as Worts and Gooderham and subsequently became Gooderham and Worts on the death of James G. Worts, at which time his son, James G. Worts Jr., was taken into the partnership. It was the third son of William Sr., George Gooderham, born in Norfolk, England in 1830 just before the family emigrated, who eventually became the central figure in the management of the firm of G&W and he became its President when it became a stock company. Although the Gooderhams were millers, wholesalers and distillers, they were not satisfied just to be connected to the Grand Trunk Railway by means of their siding. They recognized the importance of railway transportation to the development of their business in competition with the enterprises fed by the Northern Railway of Canada and with George Laidlaw providing his energetic promotional zeal, they made it their business to further their interests through the Toronto, Grey and Bruce and most immediately, by means of the Toronto and Nipissing Railway and later on by means of the Credit Valley Railway.

By the time the Toronto and Nipissing opened to Uxbridge in 1871, William Sr. was already 81 years of age and the family firm was really in the hands of his son George and his nephew James G. They were both directors of the Toronto, Grey and Bruce and spent much time campaigning for funds for both railways. Initially, George Gooderham was also a director of the T&N and there is a note in the 1877 minutes that he was resigning in favour of William George Gooderham, his eldest son and grandson of William Sr. George Gooderham's function on the T&N board was undoubtedly to keep an eye on things,

William Gooderham, Jr., born England 14 April 1824, died Toronto 12 September 1889, Fourth President and Managing Director of the Toronto and Nipissing Railway, Vice-President of the Midland Railway of Canada at the time of lease to the GTR. Metro Toronto Library Board, JRR Collection 1047

James G. Worts, Jr., born England 1818, died Toronto 1882, Partner Gooderham and Worts, Director and active promotor of the Toronto & Nipissing Railway. Metro Toronto Library Board, JRR Collection 1049

42

John Shedden, born Scotland 1829, died Cannington 1873. Railway and cartage contractor, third President of the Toronto and Nipissing Railway. Metro Toronto Library Board, JRR Collection 3715

considering that it was clearly the family's original intention to put the management of the railway into the hands of a railway man, namely John Shedden. With his untimely demise; William Jr., who had recently been appointed Vice-President and Managing Director of the T&N, became its President and Managing Director and since this provided the necessary control, George undoubtedly felt that he could relinquish this minor interest in favour of his eldest son, William George, and concentrate on the Gooderhams' considerable involvement in the banking business.

William Jr., on the other hand, even though he was the eldest son, appears to have opted out of the family business in his early years, spending his early adulthood in Rochester, New York. While the death of John Shedden was unfortunate, it probably solved a problem for the family combine and there is no doubt that William Jr. gravitated towards the family's railway interests. He remained in charge of the T&N until its merger with the Midland, at which time he and George Gox obtained vice-presidencies under the new General Manager of the consolidated Midland operation, Joseph Hickson.

As a railway enterprise, the T&N sustained two accidents throughout its short career which both held an element of the dramatic and the spectacular. The first was the tragic death of John Shedden. "Railways and Other Ways" by Myles Pennington gives us this account:

> "On May 16, 1873, he, with a number of citizens from Toronto, went up on the T&N to attend a land sale at Mr. Shedden's. On returning, he got out of the car at Cannington Station, and on attempting to get in again, while the train was in motion, his foot slipped at an opening in the station platform, and he fell between the car and the platform and was crushed to death."

Born in 1829 in Kilbirnie, Scotland, Shedden had gone to work on the Glasgow and Southwestern Railway and emigrated to North America in 1855. Following railway construction contracts in Virginia and London, Ontario, he became associated with his one-time colleague of the Glasgow and Southwestern, one William Hendrie, who had settled in Hamilton and was destined to become very prosperous with his cartage business, railway contracts and a host of other enterprises and affiliations, including a directorship on the TG&B. Hendrie had originally developed the railway cartage concept in Canada and went into partnership with Shedden, doing business with the Great Western Railway at Hamilton, London and Detroit. When the Great Western completed its stub into Toronto, John Shedden extended the cartage business to that city. In 1858, the partnership was dissolved, Hendrie taking Hamilton and all points west and Shedden Toronto and all points east, but both of them carting for both the Great Western and the Grand Trunk. When in 1862 C.J. Brydges, Managing Director of the Great Western, resigned to become General Manager of the Grand Trunk, William Hendrie was appointed cartage agent for the Great Western and John Shedden for the Grand Trunk. At the time of his death, John Shedden was also a Vice-President of the TG&B and Commanding Officer of the Grand Trunk Rifle Brigade. It was business connections such as this that facilitated concessions such as the third rail to Scarboro Junction!

The T&N Board Meeting of June 4, 1873 recorded:

> "...that this Board desires to place upon record their sense of the overwhelming loss sustained by the Company through the death of their President, the late John Shedden, Esq., a loss which is felt not only by them and by the City of Toronto, but throughout the whole Dominion of Canada and wherever his public spirit, generosity and highmindedness were known. Foremost in every good work calculated to increase the prosperity of his adopted country, he brought his sound judgement and practical knowledge to bear in all that he undertook and it must be a source of regret in the annals of this Company, that so useful a life was sacrificed through an accident upon the railway over which he so ably presided, thereby depriving the members of this Board of a most able colleague and friend."

What is perhaps surprising is that no consideration was apparently given to promoting Edmund Wragge, Chief Engineer of the road and a railwayman of considerable promise. He had begun his career as a pupil of Sir Charles Fox, became a civil engineer in 1854 at the staggeringly young age of 17, then Assistant Engineer of the Cape Town and Wellington Railway in 1859, back to an assignment as Resident Engineer of a railway in southern England and out again to Costa Rica in 1868. With his recent experience with 3′6″ railways in these countries, he arrived in Canada in 1869 at 32 years of age to accept the combined appointments of Chief Engineer of each of the TG&B and the T&N railways. In 1875 he resigned his position with the T&N to become General Manager of the TG&B and at age 46 he became the Divisional Manager of the Grand Trunk Railway based in Toronto as well as being nominally President of the Peterborough and Chemong Lake, Waterloo Junction and the North Simcoe Railway Companies.

The minutes of the September 4, 1875 annual general meeting record that:

> "The Chief Engineer having accepted the position of General Manager of the Toronto, Grey and Bruce Railway Company, tendered his resignation, which your Directors accepted and they cannot part with Mr. Wragge without expressing their regret at the severance of a connection which has existed since the formation of the Company and have great pleasure in testifying to the able and efficient manner in which the duties connected with the office of Chief Engineer have been conducted under his direction."

Unquestionably, the strength of the Laidlaw railways was the calibre of their management personnel and this somewhat eloquent minute recorded more than an ordinary business severance; obviously Wragge was held in the highest regard. What is equally evident is that the available pool of railway management talent was a fraternity and a very mobile and interlinked one. Wragge's departure was J.C. Bailey's chance. Dogged by illness, he had had to resign from the T&N as Resident Engineer in 1873. He was then already 48 years old, 12 years Wragge's senior. He must have recovered because he became Chief Engineer of the T&N and the CVR in Wragge's footsteps and in 1876 was invited to become Chief Engineer of the Lake Simcoe Junction Railway, a post which lasted until 1878 when he received a not-so-golden handshake from the President of the not-so-flush LSJR:

> "Allow me to thank you for the able manner in which you have performed your duties and to express my regret that my Company is unable to give you a more substantial recognition of them."

It would appear that it was not just illness but also a certain forthrightness that may not have endeared Mr. Bailey to the powers that were. In 1873 he appealed the decision of the T&N Board to let him go with only 3 months' salary and in 1879 there was a frosty letter of reprimand from Mr. Laidlaw after Bailey must have told William Jr. precisely what he thought of the Haggas Elevator:

> "Dear Sir: I am a little bit surprised at the letter addressed to you by Mr. Gooderham about the Haggas Elevator and will now thank you, as Chief Engineer of the Companies to give me an answer to my former letter asking your opinion thereon. It was out of delicacy for your relations with the T&N Railway Company that I gave you the option of answering or not as you chose, and therefore I think your letter to Mr. Gooderham is not in good form.
>
> Yours faithfully,
> George Laidlaw."

The point of this correspondence is that the Haggas Elevator was a controversial device and since it was invented by the T&N Railway, Mr. Bailey was obviously in a difficult position to criticize it, even though its prospectus had been sent to him in his capacity as Chief Engineer of the Credit Valley Railway.

Eventually, with the mergers of all of the lines in the 1880s with which Bailey had been associated, he became a consulting and an inspecting engineer based in Toronto, there being a reference in his papers (at the Ontario Archives) that he was the Consulting Engineer for the consolidated Midland Railway of Canada. He died in 1903 at age 78, only two years before Edmund Wragge.

In retrospect, there is no doubt that a prospectively brilliant career was cut short with the death of John Shedden at only 46 years of age and that the T&N, the Midland and the GTR lost a man who would in all likelihood have left a strong imprint on the management of all of these companies.

As for the accident that befell John Shedden, it was not unusual. In fact, the first recorded railway accident anywhere, was that where William Huskisson, a dignitary at the Rainhill Trials, was knocked down and fatally injured by "The Rocket," an accident which was similar in nature to that which occurred to Shedden. In 1879 on the Credit Valley Railway, James Gooderham, a brother of William Jr. and George, died of his injuries following a collision by a Grand Trunk engine with a special excursion car which knocked him off onto a pile of ties. Railways were an infant technology and there were a lot of things that could go wrong and put the lives of crew and passengers at risk. Employees of the railway were particularly vulnerable and those familiar with our early railway history have read countless times of the viciousness of the early link and pin couplings which would spontaneously amputate the fingers of any brakeman with slightly slow reflexes or the early uneven buffer beam heights which would mercilessly crush the unwary to death, the hazards of climbing along a swaying locomotive to squirt more tallow onto the running gear and many other hidden hazards that made countless widows and orphans overnight. An anonymous train conductor put it so eloquently over a century ago:

> "But if ever you want to feel how helpless a mortal you are in the Almighty, just get on an express engine, and get the engineer to "open everything" on a dark night. It's positively aweful to see your headlight boring into darkness, and to think that only between you and instant death there's the chance of the two pieces of iron you're travelling on being continuous and clear."

And there were other accidents on the T&N just as there have been on every railway then and now. In March 1870, some earthworks collapsed near Sunderland, burying two workers, one of them married with 7 children. On July 18, 1872, at the Little Rouge River north of Markham, the rails had been removed in order to replace the timbers on the trestle. The engine of an oncoming train crashed off the bridge and settled into the mud of the bank while the crew jumped and escaped with their lives. 18 cars were totally demolished but miraculously, the cargo of one of them, a stock car loaded with sheep, escaped unhurt.

In the same year, the passenger car of a mixed train became derailed between Wick and Uxbridge. The brakeman tried to attract the engineer's attention on top of one of the freight cars, at which point the coupling snapped, pitching the unfortunate man between the cars, "crushing him in a most horrible manner." In another accident at Scarboro Junction, a brakeman died after the wheels of a car passed over his legs. In another gory accident at Unionville in 1872, a newsboy was struck by a beam of lumber sticking out sideways from a passing train, knocking him onto the track and "mutilating his body in a shocking manner" and in yet another at Markham, a young brakeman fell between two cars and had a wheel pass over his chest. Derailments were commonplace as recalled by Mr. Robert S. Duncan, the son of John Duncan, traffic superintendent of the T&N quoted earlier in this chapter:

> "My father used to tell me that the line was very crooked, full of twists and turns and the little 4-wheel box cars had a bad habit of jumping the track. On one occasion the crew were standing around, wondering what to do about it when some farmers working in a nearby field came over to see what was wrong. After sizing up the situation one said: 'Come on boys, and lift her on'."
>
> (Burrs and Blackberries from
> Goodwood, Eleanor Todd, 1980)

The most spectacular accident to befall the T&N was of course the explosion of one of the boilers of the Fairlie engine at Stouffville. For some years, the date and location of this occurrence has been variously ascribed as being in the late 70s or the early 80s, with some locations described as "near Coboconk." The following contemporary newspaper report should settle the matter once and for all:

> "Explosion Occurred 31 January, 1874
> February 5, 1874
> On Saturday last, at 11.30 a.m., the boiler of the Fairlie engine, the best and most powerful engine on the T&NR, exploded at the Stouffville Station. The boiler, cab, and all the machinery above the trucks, were lifted completely off and the debris scattered more than 30 rods in every direction. One boiler, weighing about 10 tons was blown more than 100 yards over the station, striking the roof just over the agent's room, where it appeared to have turned end over end, tearing away the roof and the joists beneath; it then passed over the partition between the agent's room and the freight room, carrying

away the roof at the north end of the station, and landed on a woodpile about 3 rods north of the station. A joist and part of the ceiling fell on Mr. Cowley, the agent, who was at the instrument, which knocked him senseless, but inflicted no serious injury on him. Two firemen on the engine namely James Trunkfield and William Carruthers, were instantly killed. William Godfrey, the driver, was thrown against a woodpile breaking one arm and leg and dislocating his shoulder and causing such internal injuries as to prove fatal. He died on the Tuesday following. Mr. H. Haney, a wood dealer had just stepped off the cab of the engine onto the platform at the time of the explosion and was thrown several feet in the air and fell on his head and shoulders, stunning him severely and causing some abrasions on the nose and face. James Trunkfield was projected through the air, over the residence of Mr. Cowley, a distance of 22½ rods. William Carruthers, fireman and son of Alderman Carruthers, Toronto, a young man of promise, was thrown against Mr. Cowley's house, striking and smashing in the upper storey window. The concussion was so great as to completely strip him of his clothing and rendering the body one mangled mass. The sight was sad and revolting. The engine was standing about 50 feet from the station at the south end of the platform at the time of the explosion and tore away about 20 feet of the track and 25 feet of the platform. The engines were attached to the lower part of the trucks, and are not materially injured. The loss to the RR Company will be about $6,000."

Later on at the inquest, a yardman by the name of Tillson in Toronto testified that he saw Carruthers, on the morning of the accident, place a wedge over the balance of the safety valve before starting; of which he notified the driver before leaving. The evidence of Andrew Lorimer, the regular driver of the Fairlie engine, who was off duty in consequence of illness, was that it required no more skill to run the double-header than any other engine on the road. The verdict of the inquest was "that the said William Godfrey came to his death from injuries received from the explosion of number 9 otherwise known as the Fairlie engine. We also find that the explosion was due to an over pressure of steam caused by a wedge being placed over the safety valve, thereby preventing an escape of steam until a high pressure was obtained." The jury then went on to finger the real cause:

> "...also find ... gross negligence of the Company ... while the regulations require the drivers to bring loads which they cannot draw without resorting to artificial means to increase the pressure of steam."

Extract from Circular, Managing Director's Office; 15th February, 1873:

> "Enginemen and Conductors who neglect or refuse to take on their Trains the complement of loaded Cars detailed to be drawn by the Engine, (unless they have received special permission to proceed without them,) will be fined one day's pay for each offense, and in addition be disrated from 1st to 2nd class. A second offence will subject them to dismissal."

As a sidelight, an eyewitness account appeared in a letter to the *Stouffville Tribune* in 1948:

> "I was the boy who found the body of one of the two firemen, blown almost up to Stouffer's farm. The other fireman was blown into the station agent's second storey window. His house was across the yard. The engineer was blown into the end of a pile of cordwood. The brakeman went the length of the train along with the engine bell, into the caboose. The boiler went clean over the top of the station into a pile of wood. All four people were killed outright...Edward O'Brian."
>
> (Burrs and Blackberries from
> Goodwood, Eleanor Todd, 1980)

Certainly, the explosion demonstrated most vividly the awesome power of steam under pressure. As L.T.C. Rolt put it so aptly, accidents such as this drove home the message that the high pressure boilers of a locomotive were not some "glorified steam kettle" that could be tampered with at will. The coroner's jury certainly put their finger on the real cause. In the early days of railroading, boiler explosions were common and they usually resulted from eggshell-thin boiler plates, malfunctioning safety valves or lack of water in the boiler, often as a result of unreliable gauges. These occurrences were bad enough, but from the earliest days, companies were inclined to press their luck with overtaxing the capacity of their engines and the engineers were sorely tempted to squeeze a little extra out of "the old girl" by screwing or holding down the safety valves. Since the "Shedden" was virtually brand new, and had just conquered the steadily rising gradient from Berkeley Street, the verdict would have been a foregone conclusion even without the yardman's evidence.

A postscript appears in the Board minutes that "On April 1st, 1874, the Managing Director reported that he had settled with Mrs. Godfrey, the widow of the driver of the Fairlie engine blown up at Stouffville by making her a payment of $100 in full for any claim she might have considered herself entitled to."

It is probable that the poor soul was even grateful for that pittance but it certainly does much to explain how the union movement came about.

None of these accidents was ever reported to the Minister of Railways and Canals in the annual return as they should have been. This was noted in the contemporary statistical summary of returns as follows:

> "The following companies state that they have kept no records of the accidents that have occurred, viz. the Canada Southern and the Toronto, Grey and Bruce. Several others make no return, but do not say distinctly whether it was because there were no accidents or whether there was no record kept. These companies have therefore not complied with the law which requires information to be forwarded to the Board of Works within 48 hours of the occurrence of every accident and a statement duly sworn to, of all the accidents that have occurred during every six months."

In referring to management-employee relations generally on the T&N, Col. G.R. Stevens in his "History of the Canadian National Railways" made these disparaging remarks:

> "...it (the T&N) might have gone further and have become a viable property if Gooderham had been less addicted to strait jackets. But he wished the management of the line to be as precise as the rule book could make it, and so he devised an operations manual that was even more exacting than by which the railway had been built. Employees were classified, like souls in the Hindu religion in constantly ascending and descending sequences according to merit; reclassification, fines and downgrading followed automatically for even the simplest of offences, reinstatements were few and far between."

There is no doubt that all of these things happened, the company's by-laws, rule book and circulars speak for themselves, but there is nothing to suggest that William Jr. was anything but a typical employer of his day. Certainly compared to the conditions of work in the factories, being an employee of the T&N was a sinecure and comparative research with the rule books of the Grand Trunk Railway suggest similar standards. Certainly F.W. Cumberland on the Northern Railway had an equal reputation of being a tough manager and if William Jr. was given to "too much stick and too little carrot" there was very little carrot for anyone in that day and age, no matter what their occupation. What is undoubtedly true is that William Jr. came to the railway world with no training in that field and that he did what he knew best — he ran the railway just like a factory and it is easy to speculate that he would have been strongly resented on both counts. However, his disposition or lack of railway experience would have had no influence on the eventual fate of the T&N. The railway was in fact a viable property during its brief existence and the circumstances that caused it to merge were beyond the control even of much larger and more powerful railways of their day than this modest enterprise.

Cover of the only known surviving copy of the Book of Rules and Regulations. It belonged to Mr. Joseph Merrifield, longtime station agent at Cannington. Art Merrifield

A Few Enriched and Many Fleeced

It must have pained George Laidlaw no end that the catchy phrase he had coined to describe the unlucky investors with the Grand Trunk also came to be an accurate description of those who had put their faith in the narrow-gauge. Ironically, throughout its short life as an independent road, the T&N had all the traffic it could handle and it was its inability to satisfy the demands placed on it that drove it into the Midland amalgamation. It was a vicious circle of buying more cars (but not engines!) to handle the volume of traffic with increasing wear and tear on the infrastructure of the road, the rails, the freight cars, the bridges and culverts, with an increasing difficulty in timekeeping as longer and longer trains crowded this slender track.

There was also a circumstance that could not have been foreseen. In Europe, many of the narrow-gauge railway feeders have remained such to this day, but they were not part of a pioneering environment where there was an utmost pressure to squeeze every ounce of capacity out of the available resources. Their purpose was defined as a single-purpose commodity feeder (such as the transportation of slate) from the outset and by and large their environment did not change from the date of construction to the present, at least until the arrival of the tourist boom!

In Canada, on the other hand, a 3'6" gauge railway was expected to pull the same weight as a broad gauge line and a narrow gauge track which had nicknames such as "wheelbarrow tracks" or "the stump dodging line" simply did not have the capacity to cope with the onslaught of traffic. Increasingly, much freight became destined for other points by rail and all of this had to be unloaded and reloaded and the existence of different gauges simply added to the confusion and the expense of doing business, with the result that changing to the standard gauge of 4'8½" became a distasteful necessity for survival. Add the cost of making a change of such magnitude to the steadily deteriorating economy and it becomes perfectly understandable that merger was inevitable.

For a while after the opening, things had gone quite well except for the rigours of some exceptionally heavy winters and the problems of transporting all the cordwood that besieged the line. There was the prospect of the branch to Jackson's Point and surveys were in progress beyond Coboconk. A report was received by Mr. Bailey in November, 1875, quoting a price for a survey of "the extension of T&N Railway to Norland ... to include if necessary preliminary surveys, location, profile of line and plans of right of way." By September '77, a report was received that a party was 9 miles north of Minden and that "our troubles are just beginning according to the accounts of the settlers." By 1879, Mr. Bailey provided Mr. William Jr. with an estimate of $80,802 for a 12 mile extension to Moore's Falls to include stations at Norland, Elliott's Falls and Moore's Falls, with two water tanks and a 2-stall engine shed complete with turntable at the end of the line. Needless to say, this extension was never built and it is not to be confused with the Toronto and Nipissing Eastern Extension Railway project begun in 1883 which in short order became the Irondale, Bancroft and Ottawa Railway and had no connection with the T&N other than that it was backed by some of the same Toronto interests who had supported the T&N, among them Henry S. Howland, John Leys, Joseph Gray, and R.E. Kingsford.

By 1875 there wasn't really any money left over to pay for additional surveys, let alone any actual capital expenditures. By 1877 the bond interest remained unpaid and the Board was looking around for scapegoats. First of all the Province was said to have discriminated in favour of the Whitby and Port Perry Road and then the whole mess was the fault of the consulting engineer, Sir Charles Fox, who by this time could not defend himself since he had passed on in 1874. Thirdly, it was the design of the 6-wheel cars that was absolutely worthless and then the small engines originally ordered for the road "proved to be useless" and "that whatever faults there were in the construction of the road is chargeable to them." No doubt the cup of bitterness ran over since it was the call of the consulting engineers on their bond interest that, ironically, put the T&N into receivership.

With absolutely no money in the till, John Bailey's problems were mounting in the engineering department:

> "I consider it false economy to let the permanent way run down so far that the speed of the trains has to be decreased beyond the regular rate."

> "South of Uxbridge, the rails are getting pretty well worn."

> "I am aware that it is almost useless asking for a grant of money for stone culverts at this time as there is a great deal of work absolutely needed to be done and which must be done without delay."

By this time, the end was nigh and the attention of the T&N Board was riveted on the proposed purchase by the Midland Railway, which took place in July 1881. Almost immediately (November 1881) negotiations began for consolidation into the larger Midland system, with the result that the T&N annual general meeting due September 13, 1881 was postponed twice to January 17, 1882, while the general merger was ratified on December 12, 1881. The last Board meeting was eventually held on February 13, 1882 and the general merger became law on March 10, 1882 (45 Vic. Cap. 67) and effective April 1, 1882. The following were the participating companies and the signatories to the agreement:

> Toronto and Nipissing Railway, signed by William Gooderham, Jr. President and Joseph Gray, Secretary; Whitby and Port Perry Railroad, signed by J. Austin, President; Victoria Railway, signed by John Proctor, President and H.E. Suckling, Secretary; Toronto and Ottawa Railway, signed by William Gooderham, President and Joseph Gray, Secretary; Grand Junction Railway, signed by Thomas Kelso, President and William Sutherland, Jr., Secretary; Midland Railway, signed by George A. Cox, President and H. Read, Secretary.

The Lake Simcoe Junction Railway is of course conspicuous by its absence in this agreement. By the time the storm broke over its parent, the Lake Simcoe Junction had only just got into its stride with the completion of the large wharf at Jackson's Point in 1879 "and is now being used by vessels carrying cordwood." The T&N, who had never really dealt with anyone in a particularly generous spirit if the transaction involved expenditure of any sort, apparently really upset their branch line over such a seemingly minor item as officers' exchange passes. It is clear from the all-inclusive nature of the resolution that this was the straw that broke the camel's back and it is worth quoting in full:

> "*Whereas*
> the Directors of the Lake Simcoe Junction Railway Company have since the year 1873 without remuneration laboured and expended considerable sums out of their own means for the purpose of carrying bonuses and building the said railway as a branch of the Toronto and Nipissing line
> *and whereas*
> it was discovered when the people were applied to for bonuses that most of the difficulty in obtaining the same was occasioned by the LSJ Railway being projected as a branch of the T&N Railway,
> *and whereas*
> the Directors of this Company were led to believe that Messrs. Gooderham and Worts would purchase the mortgage bonds of this Company at a fair price and in fact a direct promise was made to this Company by Messrs. Gooderham and Worts to that effect
> *and whereas*
> by reason of such promise being unfulfilled, the Directors of this Company have been put to further loss and trouble;

therefore
the Directors of this Company are of the opinion that the course of the T&N Railway Company in not issuing free passes between Toronto and Lake Simcoe to the Directors of this Company is mean and ungenerous to the last degree and unworthy of a public corporation, more especially so when it is considered that by the construction of the LSJ Railway, a large and increasing traffic has been added to that of the T&N Railway. This Company is also of the opinion that in view of all the circumstances, the neglect of the manager of the T&N Railway in not obtaining exchange passes for the officers of this Company over other lines is extremely unfair and improper and this Company is determined that until such passes are forthcoming, all persons other than the officers of the LSJ Railway travelling over that line shall pay full fare and if not, that their fares shall be charged to the T&N Railway. That copies of the resolution be sent to Mr. William Gooderham, Mr. J.G. Worts and the managers of such other railways as the Executive Committee see fit. Carried, J.N. Blake, President"

In fairness to the T&N, there is a good probability that their lack of attention to this seemingly minor point could properly be ascribed to a lack of concern for the stables when the house was on fire!

There was another interesting development at the Lake Simcoe Junction Railway Board that same year, namely the addition of David Tisdale as Vice-President. This was an unusual move for two reasons. Early boards of local railways tended to draw their board members from local businessmen, bankers, politicians and others who could be of help to the venture, whereas David Tisdale hailed from Norfolk County. Secondly, Blake had been the President since 1874 and by 1878 the eventual fate of the LSJR must have been quite apparent. With the parent company in trouble, the branch had nowhere else to go and the motivation for Tisdale to take over in time for the last rites seems rather curious. However, Colonel Tisdale had a most interesting career as a lawyer, militiaman and a politician, as well as taking a special interest in railways and canals. He was an ardent supporter of the construction of the Canadian Pacific Railway and had been the moving force behind the construction of the Georgian Bay and Wellington Railway Company which was incorporated the same year as he joined the LSJR Board (1878). As it happens, the Simcoe law firm of Tisdale, Livingstone, Robb and Jackson represented Naismith and Company, the contractors working with Francis Shanly, and this certainly explains the Tisdale presence at the LSJR. One is left to speculate why he became active in the management of the railway. An obvious immediate interest would be to protect the contractors whose bonds in payment had been placed in trust because of some undisclosed dissatisfaction. (The matter must have been resolved later that year because the Board minutes of September 10, 1878 record that the LSJR accepted the road from the contractor.) If there was an ulterior motive, it was perhaps the fore-knowledge that the last of the short lines would eventually disappear and that a seat at the signing-off ceremony might just help to preserve a connection with the giant octopus.

It is not clear from the surviving records when Tisdale was appointed President of the LSJR, but an 1884 board resolution was signed by him as President, to be forwarded to the General Manager of the GTR:

"That the attention of the Grand Trunk Railway be called to the following points in connection with the management of the road hitherto:
1. By reason of the inadequate accommodation afforded for passenger traffic, much of said traffic is not only carried past the line of said railway but also carried across the line to other roads (undoubtedly

the Northern and Northwestern at Holland Landing and New-market).

2. No sufficient attempt has been made to encourage excursion business from the City of Toronto and the shareholders are convinced that if the fine natural advantages of the terminus of their road on Lake Simcoe are fairly brought to the notice of the travelling community, a large and paying traffic will be created which is now entirely lost."

Someone must have paid attention because Jackson's Point was promptly written up at length in the Grand Trunk Tourist and Resort Guide.

Although board meetings either did not take place very frequently in the 1880s or were rarely recorded, the Lake Simcoe Junction did not disappear into the Midland merger which was enacted on March 10, 1882. Article 27 of Ont. Vic. 45 Cap. 67 provided that "the agreement entered into between the Lake Simcoe Junction Railway Company and the Toronto and Nipissing Railway, set out in Vic. 42 Cap. 62, is hereby declared to be binding on the Midland Railway of Canada as consolidated," with the result that the leasing arrangement continued with the Midland Railway although the ultimate fate of the LSJR was already sealed. In 1884, the LSJR obtained power of sale (Ont. Vic. 47 Cap. 69) (at the time of the lease of the Midland to the GTR) but the leasing arrangement continued until 1892, when the following notice appeared in the Ontario Gazette and the *Globe*:

> "NOTICE is hereby given, that a special meeting of the shareholders of the Lake Simcoe Junction Railway Company will be held at the office of E. Wragge, Esq., Union Depot, Toronto, on the 25th day of October, 1892, at the hour of 2:15 p.m. for the purpose of considering and approving and or disapproving of an agreement between the Grand Trunk Railway of Canada, the Jacques Cartier Union Railway, the Montreal and Champlain Junction Railway Company, the Beauharnois Junction Railway Company, the Midland Railway Company of Canada, the Peterborough and Chemong Lake Railway Company, the Lake Simcoe Junction Railway Company, the Grand Trunk, Georgian Bay and Lake Erie Railway Company, the London, Huron and Bruce Railway Company, the Galt and Guelph Railway Company, the Brantford, Norfolk and Port Burwell Railway Company, the Wellington, Grey and Bruce Railway Company, the North Simcoe Railway Company, the Waterloo Junction Railway Company and the Cobourg, Blairton and Marmora Railway Company, for the purpose of amalgamating the said Companies into one Company under the name of the Grand Trunk Railway Company of Canada, on the terms and conditions in said agreement set forth.
>
> By order of the board,
> J.R. Bourchier,
> Secretary
> Dated this 22nd day of September, 1892."

This consolidation was ratified with the passing of the 1893 Grand Trunk Act (Statutes of Canada, Vic. 56 Cap. 47), effective April 1, 1893 and the last little vestige of the Laidlaw empire had vanished.

In the amalgamation process which began with the 1882 Cox consolidation, three significant things happened which were most important from an operations point of view.

Firstly, of the six amalgamating companies, only the T&N was of the 3′6″ gauge, all the others were 4′8½″, so the regauging of the T&N was a priority as a prelude to the newly acquired valuable Peterborough-Toronto link. The section from Scarboro Junction to Lorneville Junction therefore had a third rail added in time to permit the first through passenger train from Peterborough to Toronto to be run on December 15, 1881 via Millbrook, Lindsay and Lorneville. The Lorneville to Coboconk section was not changed to 4'8½" until August 15th, 1883 and the LSJR not until October 26th, 1883, at which point the 4'8½" gauge was in operation throughout the system and the third rail was then lifted from Lorneville right through to the old depot at Berkeley Street.

Secondly, the reader will have discerned that a Peterborough to Toronto train via Millbrook and Lorneville was not exactly as a crow might have flown to Toronto and this is where the second operational improvement came in. The charter of the projected Toronto and Ottawa Railway was used to fill in four missing gaps in the new empire. At first this was to have included the most easterly section, but this was soon dropped when the Grand Trunk took control in 1884. The first of the remaining links was a nine mile stretch from Bridgewater Junction (Madoc) to what is now Actinolite, which was opened in 1882 (and abandoned in 1894). The second section was a six mile cut-off between Manilla on the Whitby, Port Perry and Lindsay Road to Blackwater Junction (Wick), opened in early 1883. The third and most onerous section was the 14 mile "Missing Link" between Peterborough and Omemee which abounded with sink holes and labour troubles which proved to be the toughest assignment of John Bailey's chief engineering career. It was finally opened for traffic on January 1, 1884 and spelt the gradual decline of "the Old Road" between Millbrook and Omemee until its abandonment on September 25, 1927. (The fourth adjustment gave the Grand Junction Railway direct entry into the Midland Station at Peterborough across the Locks Bridge over the Trent.)

Perhaps the least heralded operational decision was conversion of the Midland locomotives to the burning of coal. The T&N stable of engines had to be replaced anyway as they were narrow gauge, but the Midland engines were brand new after the conversion of their gauge from 5'6" to 4'8½" in 1874, so that the Midland empire had incurred substantial alteration costs to keep the system up-to-date.

As for the Midland merger itself, it has never been established whether the consolidation was initially made solely to preserve Peterborough's transportation link, or whether it was an ambitious plan to create a third railway system in Ontario, conceivably joining forces with the N&NW in a united link to the proposed transcontinental railway; or whether it was a calculated move engineered by the Grand Trunk from the start. Colonel J.R. Stevens, in his "Sixty Years of Trial and Error," points out that Sir Henry Tyler, President of the Grand Trunk, headed the reorganized London Committee of the Midland and that most of its other members were Grand Trunk nominees. It is quite possible that the merger was initiated by Cox with the salvation of Peterborough in mind but at the end of the 1870s, the Grand Trunk was unquestionably at the crossroads; not only over the ruinous competition with the Great Western but the signal threat of the CPR with its Ontario and Quebec Railway poised to strike at the very heartland of the Grand Trunk dominance of Central Ontario. With stakes such as these, the Tyler-Hickson team knew exactly what had to be done. The Great Western had to come into the fold, the CPR had to be blocked at all costs from acquiring the ready-made Midland system (also financed by British investors) and lastly, the Northern and Northwestern system could not be allowed to tap into the transcontinental railway as an independent road. From the Grand Trunk's point of view, their objectives for the 1880s were all mapped out before them.

Whatever the original motivation, Cox had performed a most valuable service in rescuing the struggling lines to ensure that there was something for the Grand Trunk to take over after they had put the Great Western acquisition to bed. Of the Midland components, the T&N was, comparatively speaking, as healthy or even more healthy than the others, narrow gauge and all, when Cox set about breathing some life back into the PH, L&B even despite Von Hugel's valiant struggle to keep the road going.

Adolph Von Hugel of Pittsburgh had acquired the Port Hope venture in 1872 when he took over the road from D.E. Boulton of Cobourg and guided it through a change of gauge and the vicissitudes of the '75 slump. However by 1878 he was at the end of his tether, both physically and financially and at this point Cox made his move.

George Albertus Cox had come to Peterborough as a young man and had built his career as the local agent for the Canada Life Assurance Company. He had also started a store and was, as well, the local agent for the Canadian Express Company. He had learned to operate a telegrapher's key in his youth and gradually extended his sphere of influence both financially and politically, serving repeatedly as the Mayor of Peterborough. On his life insurance rounds he had quietly bought up blocks of Midland Railway debentures for a few cents on the dollar until he was the largest single bond holder outside of the Bank of Montreal. At this point he assumed control of the Midland Railway and deftly engineered the consolidation of the other roads serving the Lindsay-Peterborough axis. (The value of the T&N was of course the prospect of direct access to Toronto.) This assembly into the Midland Railway of Canada system proceeded very quickly and by January 1st, 1884, the new Midland was in turn transformed under lease into a division of the GTR. The old Midland Board met for the last time on May 8, 1884, at which time the lease to the GTR was ratified; the control of the road passing in turn from Cox to Tyler and Hickson, with Cox and William Gooderham Jr. remaining as Vice-Presidents and capable managers hand-picked by Cox in the key spots:

Arthur White	Traffic Manager
Harry Read	Secretary
J.G. Macklin	Chief Engineer

As the final notice published by the LSJR intimated, the Midland lease continued to 1892 with the road known as the "Midland Division." An 1886 timetable describes two "main lines," one between Toronto, Uxbridge, Lorneville Junction, Orillia and Midland; and the other between Toronto, Blackwater Junction, Lindsay, Peterborough and Port Hope. Then there were five "branches," namely the Lakefield Branch, the Whitby Division, the Haliburton Division, 'Lindsay and Coboconk' and the Sutton Branch.

When the Grand Trunk acquired the road outright in 1892, the territory became the 8th, 9th and 10th Districts, the 'Midland' identification being lost altogether (until it resurfaced partially as the 'Midland Subdivision' from Lindsay to Midland in CNR days) and the hopes and dreams of a generation of railway pioneers faded into history.

As for George Laidlaw, he did not live to see the final vestiges of his enterprise plucked away into the large combines that he had so vigorously sought to avoid twenty years before. We tend to think of rapid changes only occurring in this day and age, but the period from 1870 to 1890 saw the transformation of a countryside with bucolic charm and a newfangled form of transportation to an agrarian and industrial complex that was to form the backbone of Ontario's economic supremacy in Confederation for the next 80 years. In his later years, George Laidlaw had been plagued with the difficulties of setting the Credit Valley Railway on its feet. In truth, the project had been started too late, although ironically it was to become the most enduring of all the Laidlaw railway ventures in eventually forming the CP mainline through Ontario from Toronto to St. Thomas. The Credit Valley had been designed as another narrow gauge project but was built as a standard gauge line when in 1874 the Province of Ontario decided that in order to obtain a government grant, a railway had to be built to a gauge of 4'8½" in the interest of standardization to this gauge. This effectively ended the narrow gauge era and construction of the short line Victoria Railway proved to be Laidlaw's last and toughest project. The CVR was constantly in a financial bind. A crucial supply ship sank in mid-ocean, postponing construction and allowing the Hamilton and Northwestern Railway to attract the local traffic from Milton, Cheltenham and Inglewood, and aside from the legal wrangles about entry into Toronto, the shortage of funds culminated in a strike for arrears of wages in 1880 which further injured the health of a man who had endured the stresses and rigours of campaigning for funds, promoting his railway concepts and enduring the fiery furnace of criticism and opposition. With the completion of the CVR he disposed of his railway interests, and retired in quiet seclusion to his property at Coboconk. In 1885 the prominent citizens of Toronto wished to make a ceremonial presentation in recognition of what he had accomplished for the development of Toronto, but he graciously declined, having this to say:

"If the directors and other supporters are disappointed at our failure and inability to keep the lines we built independent and specially subsidiary to the interests of Toronto, we all have some consolation that we have greatly cheapened the building of railways, that the city expanded beyond our sanguine expectations and that directly and indirectly some of our lines led to the construction of other roads not contemplated up to that time."

And with that rearward glance, he then spoke of the future:

"Here let me add that Toronto will not enjoy nor reap the full measure of its enterprise and great investment of railways, nor will the country concerned until there is a commodious passenger union depot and ample train provision made on the Esplanade for all the railways."

At that, he withdrew into obscurity to enjoy the sunsets across Balsam Lake until death quietly overtook him four years later.

Ontario Heritage Foundation plaque dedicated to George Laidlaw in 1979 at St. Thomas Anglican Church, Balsam Lake. **Author**

An historic shot of one of the Uxbridge car sheds. Note the third rail, which dates this picture as having been taken sometime between December, 1881 and late 1883. Uxbridge-Scott Museum

THE RAILWAY

Stouffville Junction

Despite the fact that both the Toronto and Nipissing and the Toronto, Grey and Bruce Railways shared the same 3'6" gauge and had their depots along Toronto's waterfront, there was no physical connection between them that has come to light. Such a link would have been useful for through passengers and the usual exchange of rolling stock but it would not have been of value for freight, since the object was to bring it to market in Toronto. Also Berkeley Street was some distance away from the other downtown facilities.

Why Berkeley Street? Well, the enterprise being sponsored by Gooderham and Worts, and bearing in mind that this was a colonization project and in competition with the Northern, the natural thing to do was to place the railway terminus close to one's own facilities, namely the distillery and wharf. However, just as George Laidlaw had urged, the eventual consolidation of the various early downtown Toronto railway termini into one union depot was inevitable as a result of the gradual series of mergers into what is now the CNR and the CPR. The ultimate fate of the Berkeley Street Station was of course linked to the Midland consolidation.

At first it was the pride and joy of the T&N, a substantial building as befits a flagship station with ample room for freight and baggage and facilities for the travelling public. It sat at the foot of Berkeley Street on the east side, hard by the Esplanade but to the west of Parliament Street and just to the north of the original Grand Trunk right of way in the days when the tracks ran along the Esplanade. The station area is now the New Market Lane Public School grounds and the last remaining traces of the old Grand Trunk right of way along this section of the Esplanade have finally disappeared.

As the traffic on the T&N grew, the railway acquired its own wharf in 1872 "from which timber brought into the city on their cars, may at once be tumbled off into the water for formation into rafts for exportation. The structure is about 300 feet in length and about 25 feet wide, built on piles and covered with thick plank and two tracks, one along each edge. It runs at a south-westerly angle at about 30° to the Esplanade and ends in line with the east side of Berkeley Street, thus covering the whole front of the station."

This pier survived the Midland merger but had disappeared by the turn of the century with the gradual landfill extensions to the south of the GTR tracks.

In the early days of the T&N, there was only one station between Berkeley Street and Scarboro Junction and that was the original GTR Don Station which sat at the very easterly extremity of Mill Street, to the north of the main line. As the suburbs to the east of the Don River grew, stations became established at "Queen Street East" (to become Riverdale Station by 1910) and at Danforth and Main Streets, originally called "York" but changed on June 25, 1922 to "Danforth."

As has been noted, the T&N had running rights by means of a third rail to Scarboro Junction, at which point the T&N enterprise parted company. The original Scarborough station on the GTR had been located further east at what is now approximately the intersection of Eglinton Avenue and Markham Road, but the railway had difficulty restarting the locomotives on the heavy grade. A new stop was accordingly decided upon at what is now "Scarboro Junction," where a handsome station building was erected. A considerable area was laid out in lots and a post office opened in 1873, all of which attracted what was to remain for several decades the most popular settlement of the township, having a smithy, store, school, Temperance Hall, a Methodist Church and no less than 40 homes. (The original Scarborough station stop did not disappear altogether but survived as a minor halt in various locations until the end of the Grand Trunk era.)

One might well suppose why a Toronto entrepreneur anxious to build his very own railway into the hinterland would not start the strike north until Scarboro Junction. While there is no surviving record on this point, it is fair to suggest that the economy-minded Mr. Gooderham would not want to duplicate what had already been done and thus came to an arrangement with the Grand Trunk "to carry him out of town" until the terrain became somewhat easier going. Whether this involved any sacrifice in principle in view of the general distaste in Toronto for the octopus from Montreal is not recorded for posterity but certainly this détente was a practical compromise. Not only did this save duplicated earthworks for several miles but a student of topographical maps of the area may observe that the chosen route north also neatly avoided any bridging that would have been made necessary by the Don or the Rouge Rivers and this was in keeping with the declared character of the road as described by Trout in the Railways of Canada 1871:

> "It is fortunate that the route of the railway runs through a most favourable country. There are really no heavy works on the line; the rolling character of the country in the township of Uxbridge necessitates a good deal of excavation. The average number of yards of earthwork is 9,000 yards per mile. The only bridge of any size between Toronto and Uxbridge is that over the River Rouge, near Unionville, in the township of Markham, and which consists of three spans of 44 feet each, and four spans of 16 feet each, the whole structure is founded upon rock elm piles. The bridge over the northwest bay of Balsam Lake, near Coboconk, is the largest structure on the road; it has three spans of 106 feet each and 5 of 32 feet, being a total length of 478 feet. The other bridges which are already executed are, three small bridges in the township of Scarboro, all over the Highland Creek or its branches and two more over feeders of the River Rouge, in the township of Markham. There will be three small bridges in the township of Brock, over the Beaver Creek; and with the exception of a trestle bridge at Markham, seven spans of 20 feet each and a few short trestles of three spans of 16 feet each, here and there, this constitutes the whole of the bridge-work.

By the time the Toronto and Nipissing arrived to plough straight due north just to the west of what came to be known as Midland Avenue (named after the Midland Railway), Scarborough had grown from an infant rural settlement 50 years earlier to a vigorous farming community. The prospect of a railway through "the northern reaches of the township" appealed to the citizens and Mr. Worts had no difficulty obtaining his bonus in this quarter. Included in this encouragement from the township was a happy boost for the village of Agincourt which had its beginnings in 1858 with a scattering of houses along Sheppard Avenue between Kennedy and Brimley Road. The community was named after the famous French battlefield immortalized in Shakespeare's "Henry V," apparently at the pleasure of someone who pulled the right strings to obtain its post office.

In voting $10,000 for the Toronto and Nipissing bonus, the Scarborough Councillors were already familiar with the benefits of the Grand Trunk line constructed some sixteen years before and lucky Agincourt was eventually to have two stations with the coming of the Ontario and Quebec Railway 14 years later. The Agincourt Station sat for over 100 years on the west side of the line just north of Sheppard Avenue and it was only demolished in 1978 after the Scarborough Historical Society decided that it was in too poor a condition to be moved as a historic building, which is indeed what it was.

It faithfully served the Agincourt commuters to the last. In its twilight days it had the familiar bus shelter appendage and now that the beaten up old frame building has vanished into history, the lights from the new shelter shine through the night as a reminder that by some miracle there is still passenger service today. In its time, Agincourt was a typical country station with all of the usual freight commodities, including grain and livestock.

From there the line continues straight northwards to the busy gravel yards at Milliken's Corners, one of the many crossroad hamlets of the last century. First settled by various crown deeds between 1798 and 1801, the community derived its name from the Milliken family, headed by one Norman Milliken who first established a lumber business in 1807. On the general site of what is today the paved platform, he had built a hotel long before the coming of the railway. Milliken (or Millikens) first appeared in the GTR timetable by the turn of the century and has survived to this day, except that the historic little flagstop building disappeared sometime in the early 1940s. Now that ridership is on the increase from the new communities nearby, perhaps it will qualify anew for a shelter.

From there it is straight on to the brow of Hagerman's Hill and the diamond crossing at the York subdivision with the two westbound loops designed to facilitate freight traffic in and out of the MacMillan Yards.

Unionville was one of the many Ontario villages that shifted its focal point with the coming of the railway. Originally established on the 6th line north of the Rouge River, the village drifted southwards towards the railway station and was encouraged to consolidate itself south of the railway line with the coming of Highway 7 in 1920.

No doubt about it, the train made the village prosperous. It enabled the area farmers to ship grain, timber and cattle and for the population it was the convenient way to come and go. Ironically, 100 years later this is still true as the daily commuter train gets longer and longer. Unionville Station is an original T&N structure and happily the community has been determined to preserve it despite a tragic fire which somewhat damaged the westerly end of the building in 1978. Unionville has the distinctive grace of being an artist's delight in typifying a late 19th Century Ontario railway village scene, with the Stiver elevator in the background. Those fortunate enough to possess a painting of the station scene are indeed lucky.

From Unionville, the line swings east to Markham and bobs along with the contour of the land. Past the 7th line, the rails cross a small creek on one of the few remaining timber trestles and approach the cluster of elevators and the yard at Markham, a village with an early beginning around 1800.

Named after William Markham, Archbishop of York, England, from 1777 to 1807 after two trial names (Mannheim and Reesorville), Markham was a hive of industry from its beginning. Populated by the Berczy followers, the Pennsylvania Germans and by a number of British and American families, the first half of the 19th century saw the establishment of a thriving industrial hub including two tanneries, saw and grist mills, a general store, furniture and cabinet making, an early pottery, blacksmiths shops, carriage works and a wagon factory which was eventually producing horsedrawn streetcars for Toronto. With all of the manufacturing activity, Markham was known as the "Birmingham of Ontario." Those employed in these industries required homes and services so there were also carpenters, masons, bricklayers, merchants, tailors, shoemakers and innkeepers among the village population. Small wonder then that the Toronto and Nipissing project received an eager hearing. The township promptly offered a bonus of $30,000 and at a meeting in the village to give area inhabitants an opportunity to buy stock, $4,000 worth was sold at one sitting. Since the shares sold in $100 denominations, and since such an amount was a small fortune in those days, that represented 40 articles of faith which meant far more than the vote for the bonus which came out of the pockets of all of the taxpayers of the township. Not that everyone by any means was in favour of the railway. There were those who felt that it would destroy the self-reliance and the social fibre of the community and the matter was not resolved without debate.

The railway stimulated local industry and consolidated the general prosperity of the village. The farmers shipped hogs, wheat, barley, cattle, hogs and later milk. The local industries shipped their products and the railway brought in whatever was new and different. For half a century it was Markham's life-blood and made an important contribution to assuring a prominence long after economic patterns had shifted when local industries started to succumb to outside competitors. Indirectly the railway played a role in the 1871 prophecy that "Markham may ultimately become an important suburban town to Toronto," one of the few railway boom predictions that could be argued as having come true!

61

As the right of way crosses the highway and swings north to Stouffville, a touch of history remains near the 16th Avenue road in the form of a very short remainder of an embankment which supported a contractor's spurline to a nearby gravel pit which has only recently started to be filled in — the gravel of course provided the original ballast for the Markham-Stouffville section of the line.

Stouffville, the next village on the line, was somewhat different in character, being a crossroads community rather than a manufacturing base, even though the origins of Markham and Stouffville are remarkably similar, Stouffville being founded by one Abraham Stouffer who emigrated there from Pennsylvania in 1804. This community too developed rapidly as a rural market centre before the coming of the railway. The Post Office was opened in 1832 and there was the usual assortment of sawmills, gristmills, cooperages and a tannery as well as many other businesses such as foundries and also a cheese factory. However, despite all of this activity, the village developed into more of a trade centre with its strategic location on the Markham-Uxbridge road and the town line and there were stage lines connecting the village with Whitby, Uxbridge, Newmarket and Markham. With all this traffic, there were travellers to be accommodated and thirsts to be slaked, with the result that there was also a thriving hotel trade.

Interestingly enough, the original station, along with all of the other stations on the line, had already been built before the rails were laid. The design of the second Stouffville Station also deserves comment. Those familiar with Canadian railway station design will recognize it as being very similar to one of the standard CPR patterns and specifically similar to that used for the stations on the Havelock Division. Since the building familiar to all of us as the Stouffville Station was in fact the second one built in 1886 and since this is the construction period of the Ontario and Quebec Railway which preceded acquisition by the CPR, we are left to speculate as to whether the station that we know was built by an artisan who was also building the stations just to the south at Claremont and Locust Hill. It seems unlikely that the two patterns should be total coincidences but unfortunately many of the early Stouffville archives were lost in the disastrous fire of 1971 and the truth is likely to remain a mystery. Incidentally, the original station burnt to the ground early in the morning of April 23, 1886. Its design is unknown, but since all of the original T&N stations were of the same pattern, at least as far as Lorneville, it is reasonably safe to assume that it resembled the others.

At any rate, in 1877 Stouffville's position as a trade and communications centre had been enhanced by the arrival of the Lake Simcoe Junction Railway which had its southerly terminus at Stouffville. Needless to say, this made Stouffville officially "Stouffville Junction" with all of that extra status and civic pride that such a facility bestowed in its time. The loss of the first station was a chance to provide more freight accommodation, if not more passenger space as well, aside from permitting the agent to live on the second floor, thus ensuring that he would always be available to cope with the very heavy demands that would have been made on his time. Also, the junction called for an engine house, turntable and water tower, all providing extra jobs and a boost to the economy through the exchange of the additional traffic. In the case of Stouffville, all of these facilities were located just to the north of the station building on both sides of the track. The actual junction point is just barely discernible today as the Lake Simcoe track diverged to the left just at the northerly end, where the siding track rejoins the mainline. If one walks through the little copse, one will note a remarkable flatness of the terrain equivalent to the width of a road bed until further progress becomes completely blocked by a local water reservoir. Another track alignment which has become completely obliterated with the passing years is an old spur line which branched off a hundred years ago from the main line just south of the Ballantrae switch and, curving around behind the station, crossed the main street of the village to serve a tannery and other industries in the vicinity of what is still called Mill Street today.

Aside from its role as a junction point, Stouffville has another interesting claim to railroad fame. In 1879, the Brothers Barkey who had opened a foundry northeast of the station, started to manufacture a device known as the "Haggas elevator" for watering locomotive tenders. The claimed advantage was that the engine could stop on a bridge over a stream or any subterranean tank of water, lower a hose and turn on the steam from the boiler, which would then cause the water to be drawn into the tender through this device. It received a considerable amount of publicity at the time and was adopted by a number of local railroads, including such neighbours as the Northern Railway of Canada and the Credit Valley Railway. The designer was Joseph Haggas, motive power superintendent and Mechanical Engineer of the T&N who presided over the Uxbridge Shops (and who incidentally had been in charge of the locomotive on that fateful day in Cannington in 1873).

Here was an opportunity for the T&N to make its name in the railway world and William Jr. lost no time in promoting it far and wide. All the more tantalizing then, that we do not know what flaws John Bailey saw that earned him the stern Laidlaw rebuke. Certainly, if everything that was claimed for it was true, it could have been a revolutionary invention, because its advantages are indeed obvious and tempting. However, here is what Mr. R.J. Corby, Curator of the National Museum of Science and Technology had to say about its probable drawbacks:

> "I would think the system relying as it did on boiler steam would be rather wasteful of fuel. Another point is that the raising of the water temperature in the tender would reduce the effectiveness of the locomotive's injectors since the colder the intake of water the more efficient these devices are. In fact they will not operate at all if the water supply is heated in excess of about 150°F. No doubt falling water tables associated with increasing population density and industrialisation coupled with the difficulty of maintaining underground reservoirs also militated against the system. I think though that the real problem was that the device appears to have been restricted to a 4" discharge pipe giving (probably optimistically) a flow of 450 g.p.m. which in turn would depend on the engine's boiler pressure. If this were low, the flow would be correspondingly less and it is not unrealistic to anticipate a situation where the locomotive arrived at a cistern low on water and steam and be unable to take on the former. This of course would never happen with gravity tanks which were generally fitted with 8" discharge pipes giving a flow (depending on head) at least five times greater."

First page of a circular letter advertising the benefits of the Haggas water elevator. Ontario Archives (Bailey Papers)

As for the railway at Stouffville, the sidings remain but the station has gone despite a community bid to save it. With a wayfreight and a commuter passenger train that actually makes the trips twice daily in each direction since it originates in Stouffville but is stabled at Union Station the track sees quite a bit of action for an Ontario branch line in the 1980s. With the withdrawal of the VIA train, the passenger service is to be taken over by GO-Transit and it is fitting in an ironic sort of way that the Ontario Government which financed this railway handsomely in the first place, should step in and give the train service back to the people. At least the remaining descendants of those who bought stock in the line will have the consolation of knowing that their great-grandfathers did not waste their money after all!

In the meantime, to the longsuffering patrons of the "Stouffville Bullet"; a service, by the way, that had been abandoned by the CNR on January 31, 1962 and was reinstated as far as Stouffville by order of the Canadian Transport Commission as recently as June 28, 1971; we offer this humorous anecdote from the *Markham Economist* of 1873:

> "Just as the passenger train on the T&N was clear of Unionville, and running at the rate of twelve miles per hour, an old man suddenly leaped up from his seat, rushed to the platform and bounded off, turning about 40 somersaults before he brought up against the fence. In a short time he appeared at the depot, looking all around and then exclaimed: 'What an old fool! I thought I left my umbrella here, and jumped off the car to get it; and now, hang me if I don't remember chucking it under the seat'."

Ah these commuters, absentminded and impulsive perhaps, but they sure do have style!

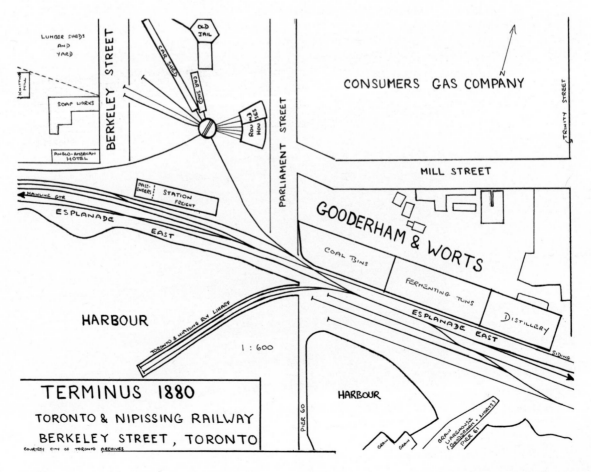

TERMINUS 1880
TORONTO & NIPISSING RAILWAY
BERKELEY STREET, TORONTO

A magnificent aerial view looking east along the Esplanade from Princess Street. In the middle of the picture is the old Berkeley Street Station, now a Grand Trunk freightshed. Behind and to the right of the station building is Parliament Street, then Gooderham and Worts' plant and distillery and at the water's edge, their commodious warehouse. Other than the station itself, all the other T&N buildings, namely the 6-road engine house, turntable and the two carsheds have given way to a freight yard and the plant of the Consumer's Gas Company. July 1894. Metro Toronto Library Board

65

The old G&W distillery building and the GTR siding. ca 1907 City of Toronto Archives (The James Collection)

Queen Street East or Riverdale Station, ca 1910. The view is looking north, with DeGrassi to the left. At that time the railway crossed Queen Street and the street car tracks at grade. Shortly afterwards (1913) the tracks were raised to pass over Queen Street to relieve traffic congestion and to forestall the increasing risk of a spectacular accident. City of Toronto Archives (The James Collection)

York (Danforth) Station looking east from the Main Street bridge. The station foundation is still visible today. The building was removed some time after closure of the station in the late 1950s. Metro Toronto Library Board

Scarboro Junction Station seen here ca 1905. The "T&N" branches off behind the building to the left. Dave Spaulding

Scarboro Junction in its later years (2 January 1957). This historic building burnt to the ground in the early hours of Sunday, December 18, 1960, taking with it many Christmas parcels ready for local delivery. Hubert Brooks

#674 switching cars at Scarboro Junction one lazy summer's day in 1940. This engine was eventually used for motive power on the CNR Museum train. J. William Hood

#2117 southbound approaching the Danforth Road crossing with her wayfreight one fine day in 1940.
J. William Hood

Sheppard Avenue East in 1940, looking towards downtown Agincourt. J. William Hood

A contrast study in passenger rail transportation 1890 - 1980 crossing under the same CPR overpass just south of Agincourt Station. Hubert Brooks & Author

Agincourt GTR in its heyday, looking north. A postcard view from the first decade of this century. Richard Schofield (Scarborough Historical Society)

Looking north at Steeles Avenue ca 1917. Markham District Historical Museum

A snowplough derailment on Hagerman's Hill, March 17, 1904. In a successive rapid thaw and freeze, the molten snow between the rails would become solid ice without allowing for the depth of the wheel flanges necessary for passing equipment to remain on the rails. The result here was a badly slewed plough and a locomotive that had to be towed back to the metals. Mrs. Pat Phillips

Unionville ca 1910, **Tony Murphy**

Unionville in 1978 just before a fire at the west end of the station which cast a cloud over its future. Happily the damage was repaired and it is to be hoped that this centenarian will continue to serve its community for many years yet. **Author**

The Rouge River trestle before replacement (looking north). Tony Murphy

The new bridge span for the Rouge River trestle just east of Unionville being lowered into position. The Grand Trunk embarked on a major renewal program of locomotives, stations and facilities between 1900-14 and it is probable that this replacement dates from this period. Mrs. Pat Phillips

A good old-fashioned pile-up at Gormley's Curve ca 1908. The spire of the Unionville United Church is visible in the distance. Accidents such as this unleashed a terrible force of destruction, shearing frames and trucks right off the bodies, even causing axles to fracture and scattering debris in an unrecognizable tangle of twisted steel and splintered timber. **Mrs. Pat Phillips**

Magnificent CN 6167 with a railfan special approaching the grade crossing at the 7th line from the west. 7 May, 1961 **James A. Brown**

Farm implement delivery day in Markham Village ca 1900. The view is of the east side of Main Street, north from where the Scotiabank building (which took the place of the store to the right of the picture) is today. Markham District Historical Museum

A different view of Markham Station in the horse drawn days. ca 1900? Markham District Historical Museum

A traditional postcard view of Markham Station, looking towards Toronto. Wilf Anthony, Toronto Postcard Club

Enjoying a quiet moment between trains. Note the sign board above rather than below the eave. Ron Richards

A fuzzy but precious shot of the pay train arriving at Markham in charge of GT #235. Obviously the taker of the photo was so excited at the prospect of a pay packet that he couldn't hold the camera still! 1909 Charles H. Heels and PAC C24689

The orderboard has gone, the station is rented out, the weeds try to take advantage, the litter blows around and the spacious sidings rarely hold more than a car or two. Author

The wreck of old 94, derailed about 1 mile east of Markham on October 15, 1954 as a result of a Hurricane Hazel washout. Pacific-type engine 5136 and the baggage car turned over on their sides but no one was hurt, the engineer and firemen escaping serious injury by jumping from the cab. Markham District Historical Museum and Charles H. Heels

The rigours of an old-fashioned winter. GT2335 and train stuck for days between Markham and Stouffville as rescue equipment could not get through to free the stranded train. The engineer had to keep a fire going to stop the boiler from freezing. Date uncertain but probably either 1912/13 or 1918/19. Markham District Historical Museum

Not even the snowplough could be guaranteed to get through in some of the tough winter storms that could make the track impassable for days. This plough was stuck for days between Markham and Stouffville. Date uncertain but believed to be 1918/19. Markham District Historical Museum

Southbound train taking on water in the Grand Trunk days Wilf Anthony, Toronto Postcard Club

Depot, Stouffville

A good composite shot of the Stiver elevator, sidings, water tower and station from the golden postcard era. Wilf Anthony, Toronto Postcard Club

A portrait shot of the pot-belly stove in the Stouffville waiting room with Arthur Lehman, baggage man and John R. Hodgins, the station agent, from left to right. ca 1924 Dinty Hodgins

*A rare interior shot of the agent's office at Stouffville taken December, 1912. Note the operator's key in the bay and on the right, the press used for making copies of train orders. Through the window can be seen the Stouffville planing mill. To the left is Dean Kester (errand boy?), Fred Jennings, baggage man (subsequently to give his life in WWI), and John Hodgins, station agent.*Dinty Hodgins

Oops! GT468 had just come off paycar duty and was being turned on the Stouffville turntable (too fast!) and when the table was spragged, the engine tipped into the pit. 1896. **Charles H. Heels**

Mary Ann

The story of poor Mary Ann does not have anything like the same happy ending, if the survival of any kind of service can be called a happy ending. No one knows how the daily mixed on the Lake Simcoe Junction Railway got its nickname, but generations of residents knew it as "Mary Ann"or "Grandma's Trunk." Interestingly enough, one of the locomotives on the Irondale, Bancroft and Ottawa was apparently also called "Mary Ann" and since both lines were indirectly connected to the Gooderhams, can the reader be left to speculate about the possibilities?

The first official timetable was issued on December 10, 1877 with two mixed trains in each direction. By 1886 this was down to one mail train each way and by 1889 there was one mixed train each way. By 1910, the passenger train had been restored with one passenger and one mixed train in each direction daily but as of August 18, 1917 there was only one mixed train each way again (with regular service to Jackson's Point abandoned) and that is the way it remained until 1928. The average travelling time of 1¾ hours between Stouffville and Sutton did not vary throughout its half century of operation.

From Stouffville, the right of way veered towards the 9th line, crossing it just north of Bethesda Road and again crossing Highway 48 just north of the Bloomington Sideroad, dividing up the rectangular concessions into a succession of larger and smaller triangles. Until one reaches the Bloomington Sideroad, the right of way has now disappeared from sight as farmers bought back their grandfathers' heritage for a few dollars to level the ground and reconnect their severed fields. Mr. Eugene Lemon is one such farmer who still has the purchase agreement between his grandfather and the LSJR. He has vivid memories of the trains as they passed through the family farmland and he recalls in particular the heavy grade up to the centre line between the 9th and 8th concessions. If the engineer could make that, he could make it to the summit of the line at 1121 feet above sea level just north of the Bloomington Sideroad and then on to Ballantrae. If not, he would have to split the train and come back from Ballantrae for the coach, especially when the rails were slippery!

As soon as the railway crossed over Highway 48, it realigned its course to stay parallel with the road. The station at Ballantrae was a flagstop situated in the northeast quadrant where the rails intersected the Ballantrae Sideroad. The flagstop was a combined section house for the section foreman and the building disappeared after closure of the line.

From Ballantrae the road was steadily downhill, passing next through Vivian, a one time crossroads community at Vivian Sideroad and Highway 48, the home of Robert McCormack, mover and shaker of the LSJR and owner of the sawmill that provided the main commodity for shipment from there. The station at Vivian was located some distance north of the Vivian Sideroad on the east side. Like Ballantrae, it was a waitingroom and sectionhouse combined. A long time resident of Vivian, Mr. George Mitchell, recalls that just before the line came through the cutting and out onto the embankment before Cherry Street, there was a spurline to the east of the line with the switch facing towards Sutton for hauling out the especially fine sand for use in the locomotive sanders.

The original Vivian Station burnt down in 1919 under tragic circumstances. The section man's son had just drowned the day before and in the preparations for the funeral reception, a coal oil stove tipped over, setting fire to the freight shed. In minutes the house and station were gone, the heat being so intense that it warped the rails in front of the building.

From Vivian, the line maintains its northerly direction to the west of the highway, being for the most part easily traceable as it crosses Davis Drive and then passes through what is now the tiny community of West Franklin. The Grand Trunk register of stations identifies a stop here called "Powells." There was never even a platform here, let alone a station building, but if one flagged the train it would stop. No doubt this was a concession to the hitherto flourishing village of Franklin which started to decline when the station was built at Mount Albert. After Powells, the line swung back towards Highway 48, crossing it just to the south of the Sharon Road and then entering Mount Albert a little to the west of

King Street; a continuation of Main Street coming into the station yard. The Canadian Northern Railway came through in 1905 and since this line provided a direct link with Toronto, the days of Grandma's Trunk were numbered from then on.

Mount Albert came into two railways by accident of location, but neither was it a creature of the LSJR. Its first settlers had arrived in the 1820s and formed a community known as Birchardtown which then became Newlands and with the opening of the Post Office in 1865, the village was named in honour of the visit by the Prince of Wales. The coming of the railway meant a great deal to the inhabitants as they could now travel in comfort to Toronto, even if the journey did take all morning. Much more happily, a pleasure jaunt to Lake Simcoe was now within easy reach at moderate cost.

North of Mount Albert, the alignment continued due north just to the east of the highway with telltale sections still visible at the Queensville Sideroad. Eventually, the CN.R intersected the Grand Trunk right of way at a point about 300 yards north of the Queensville Sideroad at Mount Albert Creek, where the Grand Trunk crossed the creek and continued straight on to Brown Hill through what is now an extensive reforestation area. At that time, a crossing tower was erected for the safety of trains on both lines and a local resident recalls that the operator was a man by the name of Kennedy. No visible trace of this tower remains today. The coming of the Canadian Northern Railway through Mount Albert and the arrival of the radial cars in Sutton by 1909 had started to put a considerable dent in the traffic available to Mary Ann and on May 19, 1928, mixed train service was discontinued.

The rails on the 15 miles of track between Stouffville and Zephyr Crossing were lifted between October 12th and 25th, 1928; all except a short stub between Stouffville and Ballantrae which continued to be used as a spur for rolling stock storage for about another year or so before being removed also. The northerly section of the branch was connected to the Bala subdivision at the Zephyr Sideroad by means of a wye and from then on there was freight service only as required.

The original Zephyr station was not the same building which came to preside over the wye after abandonment of the southerly section; it was a frame building of similar design to the other original stations on the line and a local resident, Mr. Reeford Sedore, recalls that it stood on the southside of the Simmerson (Zephyr) Sideroad and disappeared sometime in the middle thirties.

The next community, Brown Hill, came into being just before the railway arrived and was originally known as Blake Station, which was reasonable since the land on which the station was built belonged to J.N. Blake, the President of the railway. Like the other stations, Blake, or Ravenshoe (after the village to the west) as it was also shown on early maps, was a good sized building but had become a flagstop when the Grand Trunk took the line over. The station had a siding until a few years ago and in the early days, the principal freight traffic came from the stockpens.

Baldwin Crossing on the other hand, had always been a true flagstop in a rather picturesque setting at a medium sized wooden trestle over Black Creek just downstream from "Devil's Elbow." The little waiting room survived into the early 1950s and then disappeared.

The right of way then continues straight as a die on the level into Sutton, the real operating headquarters and the spiritual home of the LSJR. The reader may recall that when the line was outfitted, provision was made for turntables and engine houses at Sutton and Stouffville. Scrutiny of the Sutton Branch timetables throughout the history of this line shows that the daily train originated in Sutton and this is borne out by the memories of Mr. W. Chapelle, a resident of Sutton whose father was Mr. Lawrence Chapelle, station agent until the mixed service ended in 1928. After that, he recalls, there was no need for an agent, but before then there was lots of freight from the grain elevator and the stockyards and he had to be up betimes to ensure that the engine housed in the local shed was getting steam up for the morning run. The engine shed at Sutton disappeared at the end of the Stouffville service but the manual turntable remained for a number of years until it was replaced by the wye in the early 1940s.

At the Stouffville yard, the engine house is not within the memory of Mr. Dinty Hodgins, son of Mr. J.R. Hodgins, the agent "at the other end", so it is reasonable to conclude that the Stouffville engine shed disappeared very early, although the turntable did of course remain in its stockade on the west side of the main line until abandonment of the branch. The only other full-time station agent on the branch, incidentally, during the Grand Trunk days was Mr. J.P. McLean at Mount Albert, all the other stations being flagstops, although Brown Hill also had an agent, Miss E.G. Norris, from 1919 to 1923.

Sutton also had a water tower and throughout its railway history had three stations. The first was a standard T&N design which was replaced at the turn of the century with the standard GT model. This second station was struck by lightning "in the early twenties" and since it is unlikely that the CNR would have built the third structure for a way freight service, we assume that it was erected a few years before the abandonment of the branch line. This third station fell into disrepair during the 1970s but has been rehabilitated by the Georgina Historical Society as a museum building and may now be seen at the Georgina Township Park just north of the highway between Sutton and Keswick.

The original attraction of the LSJR to the T&N was of course the prospect of being able to tap Lake Simcoe at Jackson's Point just as the Northern was doing at Belle Ewart. Because of this, it is perhaps surprising that Jackson's Point never became anything more than a flagstop in the scheme of things. Of course, by the time the LSJR got into its stride, the Midland merger was at hand with ready access to the lake at Beaverton and by the time the Grand Trunk got the property, the main industries were the resort traffic in the summer and the ice traffic in the winter. Traditionally, the only way to keep anything cool was in an icebox and this required tons and tons of ready cut ice, but with the advent of refrigerators this business melted away almost overnight. As for the passenger receipts, the resort traffic never amounted to the volume that it might have done, because of the Toronto and York Radial Company which reached Jackson's Point in 1906 and provided a competitive 2½ hour trip from its terminus at the Summerhill CPR station to Jackson's Point via Richmond Hill, Aurora, Newmarket and Queensville. It was ironic that only a few years later in the midst of the Depression, the radial cars ceased to run with the result that Sutton and Jackson's Point were then deprived of any kind of passenger railway service.

At any rate, since the value of Jackson's Point to the railway had deteriorated rapidly in the 1920s, the stretch between Sutton and Jackson's Point was closed September 24, 1927 and the rails lifted the same year. From Sutton the line had crossed Dalton Road and followed a right of way along what is now Park Road, eventually being intersected by the radial line near Metro Road, then crossing Lake Road to run down what is now a park along the east side of Lorne Road right out onto the wharf where the ice houses used to stand.

The Grand Trunk Station sat on the northerly edge of Lake Road at the "park" entrance and consisted of one of the standard GTR flagstop waiting rooms and two additional open shelters for the protection of excursionists and any baggage in the event of rain. When the railway was dismantled, all three structures were moved to the water's edge in the same park. The two open shelters have survived to this day, but the station itself succumbed to the weather and was dismantled some years later. The ice houses were taken down when the line was taken out but the wharf structure has survived as the park pier even though it has been twice lowered since first constructed for the railway.

It is only very recently that the fate of the Sutton Branch was sealed altogether when the Toronto Division Superintendent of the CNR issued the order that the switch to the Sutton Spur would be spiked as of August 13, 1979. Somewhat belatedly, Georgina Township had hoped to save the branch with plans for a steam tourist attraction but the disposal of the rails and ties had already been tendered and in mid-July, 1981 the remainder of the old Lake Simcoe Junction Railway passed into oblivion.

STOUFFVILLE STATION.

Stouffville, a busy country junction in the Grand Trunk days, with the Stiver Brothers elevator to the west and the water tower and station to the east of the tracks. Wilf Anthony, Toronto Postcard Club

Stouffville Junction with its well kept garden and freight in the sidings of a kind that has not been seen for many a year. ca 1920 Dinty Hodgins

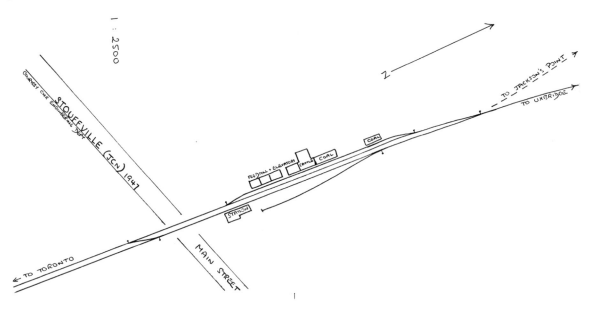

The Sutton Branch section gang at the Stouffville turntable. Note the 56 lb. rail. ca 1910 Ivan Harris

A section of 56 lb. rail from the narrow gauge days still doing duty as a barn door jam. Author

Ballantrae Station ca 1925 Left is Bert Bates, sectionman and right Dan Baker, section foreman. Markham District Historical Museum

The original railway station at Vivian looking north from the Vivian Sideroad. This station was destroyed by fire in 1919. George Mitchell

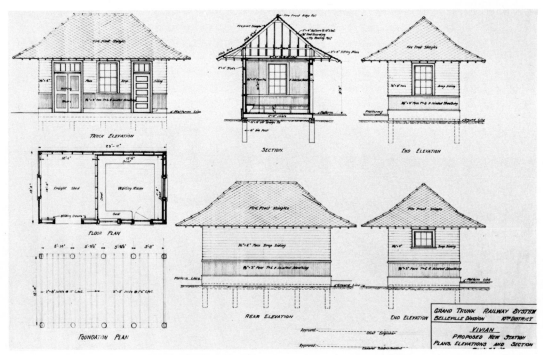

Plan of the replacement station building at Vivian, erected 1919 and demolished 1928. PAC C112119

The old Mount Albert "Grand Trunk" Station, so called to distinguish it from its upstart competitor, but actually of T&N vintage. Mrs. Gladys Rolling

Mrs. W.B. Rose at the side of the Brown Hill Station in the early 1930s. The building was demolished in 1935. The similarity to the Kirkfield Station is evident from the contour of the overhang. Mrs. Zelda Rose

Mr. Herbert Bartholomew remembers a bad snowplough accident somewhere between Ballantrae and Brown Hill in the winter of 1921/22 when the plough rode up over the frozen ice, causing the engine to derail and run off down the embankment. Mrs. Zelda Rose

The trestle at Devil's Elbow, just south of Baldwin's Crossing. **Author**

The Grand Trunk Station. Note that Sutton was called Sutton West to distinguish it from Sutton, Quebec. **Bob Luke**

Doubleheader on the snowplough at Sutton, 1910. The plough had cleared the line from Uxbridge to Scarboro Junction and on its return to Stouffville, it also cleared the Sutton Branch. The second engine had developed mechanical trouble and the only way it could be kept from freezing was to run it in reverse. Charles H. Heels and PAC C 24686

Sutton West Station.

An exceptionally detailed post card view of the (Grand Trunk) second Station. ca 1900 Hubert Brooks

The third Sutton station at its new home in the Georgina Township Park, repaired and sporting an authentic coat of paint about to start a new lease on life as a museum building at the Georgina Village Museum. Author

Game over as the rails came out at Sutton on July 14, 1981. Author

Jackson's Point Station at the height of its popularity around 1900. **Mrs. Zelda Rose**

*An annual fixture, the famous J. P. Lennox picnic to reward the party faithful on July 20, 1907 in the "park"
at Jackson's Point down by the wharf. Note the ice houses in the background.* Bob Luke

The "Enterprise" at dock at Jackson's Point wharf. She ran many passenger trips in the heyday of the line into Jackson's Point for the refreshment of hardworking folks up and down the line to Stouffville and beyond. She was the first twin screw steamer on Lake Simcoe and was a large roomy vessel of 99 tons and an 81 ft keel. After changing hands numerous times, she sank in Lake Simcoe in 1903 and the speculation is that Stephen Leacock had her in mind when he wrote "The Sinking of the Mariposa Belle". Georgina Village Museum

Jackson's Point Station shortly after closure, all set for a retired life of fresh air and fun! R.F. Corley Collection

Cutting ice. At the top of picture A there is water where the ice has been harvested. Just below, the ice has had the snow removed and a team of horses draws a plough which cuts the ice part way through by ploughing along and across. The ice was then in pre-cut blocks of about 2' x 3' and then cut into floats 4 blocks wide and about 10 blocks long (rather like a generous chocolate bar — author) and was then floated along the channel towards the ice houses. In the foreground is a man on a plank with a chisel to break off 4 block sections which were turned and floated down a narrow channel on their way to the elevator (picture B). Here they were divided into individual blocks and taken from the water by the elevator to be stored in the ice houses or to be loaded straight into railway cars. Picture C shows a whole ice cutting team grouped together with their shovels, picks, chisels and teams of horses with the elevator in the background. Mr. Herbert Bartholomew, an old-timer section man on the GTR in these parts remembers that you could earn 32¢ an hour cutting ice in the winter and 28¢ an hour working as a section man during the summer. Bob Luke

The ice loading crew taking a breather from their gruelling job. Georgina Village Museum

"Loaded by James Birch and Walter Sedore for the Lake Simcoe Ice Supply Company. Walter Sedore, James Birch, both of Sutton. Jackson's Point, August 11, 1901." Hubert Brooks

100

TORONTO AND NIPISSING AND
Lake Simcoe Junction Railways.

TIME TABLE,

Commencing at 7 a.m., Monday, December 10th, 1877, (Sundays excepted.)

TORONTO TIME.

DOWN TRAINS MOVING SOUTH.

	No. 2 Mixed.	No. 4 Mixed.	Miles from Jackson's Point.	STATIONS.	
	P.M.	A. M.			
	6.00	10.25	56	Toronto, - - - Arr.	
	4.30	8.45	27	Stouffville, -	
	3.55	8.10	21	Ballantrae, -	
	3.45	8.00	19	- Vivian, -	
	3.25	7.40	15	Mt. Albert, -	
	3.05	7.20	8	Ravenshoe, -	
	2.45	7.00	3	- Sutton, -	
	P. M.	A. M.	0	Jackson's Pt., - Dep.	

UP TRAINS MOVING NORTH.

STATIONS.	Miles from Toronto.	No. 1 Mixed.	No. 3 Mixed.
		A. M.	P. M.
Toronto, - - - Dep.	0	7.00	3.30
Stouffville, -	29	9.15	5.30
Ballantrae, -	35	9.55	6.10
- Vivian, -	37	10.05	6.20
Mt. Albert, -	41	10.20	6.35
Ravenshoe, -	48	10.40	6.55
- Sutton, -	53	11.00	7.15
Jackson's Pt., - Arr.	56	A. M.	P. M.

☞ Rules and Regulations in effect on T. & N. Ry will govern trains on Lake Simcoe Jct. Railway.

WM. GOODERHAM, Jr., Managing Director.

Ontario Archives (Shanly Papers)

101

Meeting Up With The Midland

As Trout put it so succinctly:

> "the rolling character of the country in the township of Uxbridge necessitates a good deal of excavation."

It would have necessitated a good deal more if it had been built to mainline standards; it was in this section that the advantages of the narrow gauge were exploited to the fullest extent in that the alignment has some of the characteristics of a roller-coaster track!

In all fairness, the gradient rises rapidly from 892' above sea level at Stouffville to 1102' at Goodwood Station and to 1152' at the summit of the line over Big Garibaldi (or Beaver) Hill, dropping again to 886' at Uxbridge and never exceeding 920' (Portage Road) anywhere else on the line. In fact, the summit near Goodwood is higher than any point on the Victoria Railway or for that matter, anywhere on the consolidated Midland system. Since the difficulty of the road was not only of summit level and curvature, but also of gradient, helper engines over this section were a necessity from the beginning. Unfortunately, records on this point are very scanty but older Goodwood residents can remember engineers leaving half their trains at Stouffville Junction or Goodwood and coming back for them. The same would undoubtedly apply to the heavily laden freight trains from Uxbridge. Even more fascinating is the story passed on by an old conductor, retired now for a good many years, who once offered to show Mr. George Horner, a most knowledgeable expert of CNR operations in the Toronto area, the exact onetime location of an old spur and turntable just to the south of the Port Perry Road on the east side of the track, which was reportedly used in the T&N days to turn the helper engines sent out from Uxbridge to push the trains over Big Garibaldi Hill between the 3rd and 4th concessions. If it existed, and it seems quite plausible that it might have, it was likely abandoned when the doubling siding was installed in the 4th concession, a spur with a 19 car capacity which survived until the end of steam operations.

Although the coming of the railway to this township did a lot to offset the recession by providing employment in the lumber trades and a consequent cash flow among the local businesses, it had caused a lot of political dissension. Joseph Gould of Uxbridge Village stood to gain a lot from the consequent development of the area and there was a strong feeling on the part of the township farmers that they should not have to subsidize something that would have the most beneficial effect on the Village of Uxbridge itself. According to Eleanor Todd, Goodwood's historian, the Village of Goodwood was persuaded to throw in its lot with Uxbridge Village upon the promise of a station (which Joseph Gould would certainly have the influence to deliver). In summary, the township narrowly approved the $50,000 bonus, the motion scraping through with only 43 votes to spare:

> "Railways were then new to Canada; their advantages were not understood; many honestly believed that a railway would not benefit the county, while the representatives from the east and the west opposed it because they conceived the centre of the county and the county town would only be benefited, and that to the detriment of their own localities."
>
> (W.H. Higgins, The Life And Times of Joseph Gould)

Goodwood had its own problems once the railway came through:

> "Soon trains would actually be running through Goodwood school-yard.... In twenty short years the monsters threatening the safety of the school children had switched from bears to trains, but at least this time the brutes would always cross the trail in the same place.... The iron monster turned out to be a blustering pussycat most of the time. The old Nipissing trains were very slow and the conductors didn't mind when the children jumped on for a short ride. The older kids had a game where they took a run and a jump and vaulted over the flat cars when trains were blocking the road to the school."
>
> (Eleanor Todd, Burrs and Blackberries
> From Goodwood)

In a more serious vein, Goodwood had expanded very well with the coming of the railway from a quiet village with an hotel, two churches, a school, a store and a wagon shop to a bustling community where the streets were lined with farmers' wagons waiting to unload their produce at the station, and carloads of potatoes were the order of the day. The other commodity on which the village thrived was the shipment of cordwood, somewhat to the consternation of places such as Agincourt and Markham which had trouble just getting an allocation of flatcars.

A little further up the line at the 4th Concession, a switch was put in from the mainline to a steam saw mill which went to work on 250 acres of virgin forest northeast of Goodwood.

Although the station building which was dismantled in 1960 was an original T&N station, it was apparently originally located on the east side of the tracks in company with the elevator and was moved to the west side in 1890. From 1927 to 1939 the CNR operated a spur line to their own gravel pit which branched off to the west just north of the station and re-crossed the 3rd line about half a mile north of the mainline grade crossing.

As has already been recorded, the real hoopla took place when the rails reached Uxbridge. Here no effort was spared to make the railway feel at home including the provision of a special $2,000 bonus (from the village) to secure a roundhouse and the car shops. While the main 6-stall roundhouse was at Berkeley Street, the repair of engines and rolling stock and the construction of freight cars was to take place at Uxbridge under the supervision of Joseph Haggas. The engine house held 4 locomotives and it is quite conceivable that the Midland Railway would have kept the carshops going as an extra repair facility but unfortunately in January 1883, the roundhouse and shops burnt to the ground. This ended any ambitions Uxbridge might have had as a railway centre. The carshops were transferred to Peterborough and the locomotive stabling was consolidated at Lindsay (which would have taken place in any event since Lindsay had become the focal point of the Midland network). The four locomotives destroyed in the fire were narrow gauge and were simply written off.

The original Uxbridge Station (a drawing of it has survived in the Uxbridge-Scott Museum) was another T&N job and it simply became inadequate for the traffic it had to handle. As an interesting sidelight, there is preserved in the same museum a letter written to Mr. John O'Neill, the first station agent at Uxbridge:

"Toronto & Nipissing Railway,
Managing Director's Office,
Toronto
May 12th, 1882.

Mr. John O'Neill,
Dear Sir:

Having withdrawn from the active management of the Toronto and Nipissing Railway, I have now much pleasure in presenting you with the accompanying silver watch and chain as a token of my personal esteem and as a slight acknowledgement of my appreciation of the zeal and ability with which, during the past eleven years as the first station master, you have performed the important duties assigned to you.

The many assurances which have reached me from various sources, of the satisfactory operating of the Toronto and Nipissing Railway, in the interests of all parties concerned, and the unprecedented record secured for absence of injury to passengers and property conveyed over the line, afford very gratifying proof of careful management, and of intelligent, faithful, and unceasing effort on the part of those associated with me in the several departments connected with the railway, and I trust that the Midland Railway of which the Toronto and Nipissing Railway now forms a part, and to which your services have been transferred, will continue to receive the same faithful service at your hands.

In reviewing the satisfactory results obtained, I acknowledge with pleasure the efficient and promptly rendered assistance of the officers and men composing my staff.

Accept my best wishes for your future and continued success.

Yours sincerely,
W. Gooderham"

Perhaps today, this gesture would be written off as suffocating paternalism, but for this day and age, the boss did what was expected of him and since it might be reasonable to suppose that there must have been other employees of the T&N who merited the same letter, it must have been quite a bill for silver watches and certainly no one could have been thanked more graciously for their services.

In 1904 the Grand Trunk built their new graceful "witch's hat" station which has so far survived on location as the home of the CN section foreman and the older station was relegated to a freightshed and subsequently disappeared. Over the years, Uxbridge has seen the same gradual decline in passenger and freight traffic as other rural centres but the renewed interest in localities that have the tranquility of the countryside but proximity to the city has encouraged the town to keep up a steady campaign for an extended commuter train service. Joseph Gould would have been proud.

Once on the other side of Uxbridge, the pioneering engineering problems were by no means over as the roadbed now jostled with the swampy banks of the Beaverton River (known locally as Beaver Creek) all the way north of Blackwater Junction. The Grand Trunk Railway Stations and Tariffs taking effect December 17, 1890 indicated flagstops at Marsh Hill and Wick. White's "Altitudes in Canada" shows these stations as being 3.66 and 7.92 miles respectively from Uxbridge, which would place them at the 12th concession of Reach Township and the 2nd concession of Brock Township respectively. There is a very old local notation (1882) that it was proposed to move Marsh Hill Station from the 12th to the 13th concession but since what is left of the Marsh Hill community is on the 12th concession also, this would not have made much sense unless the station had been in danger of disappearing into the bog!

The Marsh Hill Station is not recorded as such in any timetable, even in the earliest known T&N timetable of 1874 and it may well have been little more than a waiting room, if that.

Wick Station on the other hand does appear in the early available timetables of 1874 and 1880 and we are indebted to the County of Victoria Centennial History for an explanation as to its disappearance. With the construction and completion in 1883 of the section of track linking the T&N about one mile north of Wick with the Whitby, Port Perry and Lindsay railroad, thus affording a direct run from Lindsay to Toronto in the Midland amalgamation, the original Wick Station and the station at Cresswell (which was called Manilla) just south of the new easterly junction point, became redundant and were abolished in favour of new stations at Wick Junction and Manilla Junction respectively. The name of the former was then changed to Blackwater Junction but for those who delight in historical quirks, the call sign for Blackwater Junction remained WK until the abandonment of service.

With the creation of the junction, a small village grew up around the railway, with grain elevators, stockyards and a sawmill, all of which brought in the surrounding farmers to do business. Just south of the road leading to the station were stockyards of considerable size and until the advent of trucks, the shipment of cattle, hogs and sheep were very heavy. The station itself was a large frame building. It had two waiting rooms, one each for ladies and gentlemen, a ticket office, a baggage room and a restaurant which was established when the Grand Trunk took over. (During the T&N days the passengers were fed and watered at Uxbridge.) Since Blackwater Junction was now an important connecting point for travellers converging on Toronto from Midland, Coboconk, Lindsay and beyond, there was inevitably waiting time and it was an approximate halfway house for most destinations. Besides, the opportunity to take on a little sustenance would divert the traveller's preoccupation with the surrounding bleakness of his environment, especially at night and on a stormy winter's day! The restaurant finally closed during the 1930s and on August 28th, 1941 the restaurant building was demolished. Blackwater Station remained unaltered throughout its life. The agency was removed with the discontinuance of passenger trains in 1962 and the building was torn down a few years later.

With the simultaneous creation of Blackwater and Lorneville Junctions with their wye facilities by 1884, the flexibility of the Midland System was enormously enhanced. First and foremost the passenger service was now from Toronto direct to Lindsay and Peterborough and on to Port Hope and Belleville. Passengers from all points originating at Midland came through Lorneville Junction to catch connecting trains at Blackwater Junction in either direction. The direct Toronto to Coboconk service of the T&N days was gone for good, Coboconk now being served by a daily mixed train from Lindsay via Lorneville Junction.

By the 1940s the passenger service operated between Lindsay, Lorneville Junction, Blackwater Junction, then returned from Blackwater Junction via Lorneville Junction and on to Midland. Gradually, the number of trains on the Midland network were phased out until, from 1956 to the end of service, the trains operated in a "scissors" fashion. Train 93 left Lindsay at 8:10 a.m. to Lorneville, became 96 to Blackwater and continued as train 93 to Toronto. Train 603 left Lindsay at 10:10 a.m. to Blackwater Junction, continued on to Lorneville and Midland. Finally, evening train 95 left Lindsay at 6:20 direct to Toronto. The corresponding trains in the opposite direction were train 92, leaving Scarboro Junction at 9:28 direct to Lindsay, train 94 from Scarboro Junction at 5:59 to Blackwater Junction, becoming train 97 to Lorneville and train 94 again to Lindsay. The afternoon train (604) from Midland operated through to Lorneville Junction and straight on to Lindsay.

As for the Coboconk mixed, it was down to Mondays, Wednesdays and Fridays during the 1940s and the coach was taken out on March 25th, 1955 and freight service ceased altogether on March 30, 1965. The service continued to be pruned until the last passenger service of any kind on the Midland subdivision were trains 94 (97) and 93 (96) which made their last runs on January 30 and 31, 1962 respectively, the equivalent Sunday trains (85, 86 and 87) ending on January 28, 1962.

The next section of the old T&N thus had become the axis on which the Midland subdivision had come to depend for integrating its service between Midland, Lindsay and Toronto. As the line swings due north from Blackwater Junction, it will follow the

Beaverton River all the way to Cannington, the next stop being Sunderland. Various sources have made reference to the fact that an alternate route had been considered through Vroomanton and that the failure to obtain the railway caused that community to decline (true for many villages that had failed to get rails in that day and age).

Sunderland is in a true sense a railway village. While the first lots had been taken up in the 1820s, growth was very slow. Originally known as Jones' Corners, real expansion came with the construction of the railway and by 1875 Sunderland had 32 businesses including a big water-driven sawmill south of the station which supplied a lot of lumber to construct the village. In the declining years the principal freight was turnips out, coal in, and the business done by the Peterborough Co-op. The station building, after sitting around in a badly vandalized condition, was finally demolished in the late 1960s.

Cannington was the largest of the Brock Township communities. The village had been established in 1835, settled mostly by Irish, Scottish, English immigrants and some veterans of the Imperial Army who helped give the fledgling village strong leadership. Cannington (named after the Honourable George Canning, a contemporary British statesman) became very much involved with the history and fortunes of the T&N. First of all, there was the matter of the bonus fight which was finally settled on March 9, 1869 with a vote 287 in favour and 123 against. The local celebration of this event was followed in short order by the official sod turning ceremony on October 16, 1869, accompanied by the usual banquet and speeches. The Premier of Ontario, John Sandfield Macdonald, who officiated, spoke to the assembly in favour of giving the railway local financial support. In the meantime, George Laidlaw had made a very profitable personal investment in the area together with the construction of the "Laidlaw House," one of the two T&N "railway hotels" and the naming after him of the street leading from the station to the main street (which in turn was named after M.C. Cameron, Provincial Secretary and also a director of the T&N), as well as the naming of Trootie Street after his daughter. Also in the area developed by George Laidlaw are Shedden, McRae and Elliott Streets, as well as Nipissing Street, the last certainly being a reference to "The Nipissing" as the railway was frequently referred to for short.

In November 1871, the rails reached Cannington and the village became a temporary terminus until completion to Coboconk a year later.

It was not long after, on May 16, 1873, to be exact, that the tragedy of John Shedden's death came to the village and in the *Globe* two days later the following appeared:

> Dear Sir,
>   I was on the platform of the Nipissing Railway when the accident occurred which terminated in the death of Mr. Shedden. To meet the wishes of his friends, I consented to commence the inquest at once and proceeded to my office in the village to obtain the necessary forms, etc.
>   On my return, I found the train had left, taking with it the body of the deceased, thus stifling all enquiry.
>   Such high-handed proceedings I consider to be injurious to my office and detrimental to all public interests. I hope that by bringing this matter before the public such indecent violation of the law will not be repeated.
>
> Cannington, May 18th, 1873
Alfred Wyatt, Coroner"

In the summer of 1968 the boarded up and derelict station building, just wanting three years to its centennial, burnt to the ground and in among the dilapidated coal houses the weeds are taking over. As the rails cross the county line into Victoria, stop signs have been placed by the right of way to have the occasional carload freight of coal into Woodville "stop, look and listen" for the road traffic that came to destroy the railway.

The township of Eldon was first surveyed in 1826 and sparse settlement began with scraggy land available at $1 an acre. The early settlers endured tremendous hardships because of the meanness of the soil but among these early clusters of human endurance was Irish Corners (after an early settler by that name) which became Woodville in 1858. The village received a shot in the economic arm with the coming of the railway and started to thrive with carriage shops, three hotels, sash and door and cheese factories, grist and planing mills and numerous other businesses. Today Woodville is a lovely quiet village set among the trees for which it was renamed and enjoys the dubious distinction of being the latter-day terminus of the T&N!

As one drives the scant two miles north to Lorneville, one can still discern the slightly elevated roadbed to the west of Highway 46, but identifying the actual junction location today is best accomplished by orienting oneself according to the slight cutting to the east of the highway where the line used to go on its way to Lindsay. What is now Lorneville, was referred to as Woodville Junction or Midland Junction in the T&N days and became officially Lorneville Junction when the GTR assumed the line. The atlas for this area recites that in 1881:

> "Lorneville has grown up around the junction of the railways, where a good deal of grain is bought. The population is mostly composed of railwaymen and their families. Near the station and other staion buildings, are two hotels, shops and the Post Office."

It is still possible to locate the diamond and the westbound leg of the wye if one asks permission to cross some private property, but aside from a rotting tie or two there is nothing left of this historic junction, save the station itself which was rescued by Mr. Elmer Jordan, a local resident, and placed on his farm as a souvenir of his railroading days. Details of the station building are a little sketchy, but the consensus seems to be that at least since the Grand Trunk days, there has only been one building which was rebuilt and gradually diminished in size as the importance of the junction started to wane. The first portion of the junction to go (other than a passing loop and weigh scale north of the diamond on the west side, removed in 1931 or 1932) was the trackage north of the diamond all the way to Coboconk in 1965. As of August 1st, 1966, the CNR abandoned the trackage from Lindsay to Beaverton East, the junction itself and the section from Woodville northwards, and the rails themselves were lifted in 1967.

When the T&N arrived at the junction, the Port Hope, Lindsay and Beaverton Railway was already in business as far as Beaverton (1871), so that the 3′6″ gauge had to intersect with the newly laid 5′6″ track. What a prize it would be if a picture of that oblong "diamond" had survived! In among the Bailey Papers there is an interesting letter from George O. Stewart, Chief Engineer of the Midland to W. Gooderham, "Manager Nippissing (sic) Railway, Toronto."

> "Port Hope, 21 March 1873
>
> Dear Sir,
>   I am desirous of drawing your attention to the necessity that exists for a semaphore at the Woodville Junction. At present there is considerable risk incurred by the trains occupying the tracks at the crossing and when the summer special trains are running, the risk will be very much increased. I hope therefore that you will have the matter attended to at once. I would suggest simply an arm worked by a handle below so as to be turned across either of the tracks as required with a lamp for night operations. If you wish, I will send for a drawing of one I propose erecting at our junction with the Muskoka Railway at Orillia.
>
>   Yours truly,
>   George O. Stewart
>   answered March 22nd, JCB"

The former PH, L&B standardized its gauge to 4'8½" in 1874 and it was not until the "Midland Merger" and the conversion of the narrow gauge, that Lorneville Junction was reorganized into the configuration remembered by generations of travellers. There are many reminiscences, some nostalgic, some unpleasant, but many humorous of the days when the train was part of everyone's life and we are indebted to the CRHA and Mr. Tom Dickson, son of the agent (Mr. Bill Dickson) for this charming vignette of rural railroading:

"You must know that the diamond was protected by semaphores a quarter mile from the station. Each semaphore was controlled by a cable which was wound onto a drum to put the signal to the "go" position. To change to "stop" the cable was let out by kicking a release cog.

One fall day, my father heard the telegraph key chatter a message that a freight train was leaving Lindsay for Midland. To be sure, dead sure, that the signal was clear, he went to the station platform to check. The chain was wound tight on the drum, the signal arm was straight up, the light was green.

A little later the train whistled repeatedly. My father heard it but, knowing the signal was clear, he thought of cattle on the track or some other reason for the whistling. A few minutes later the train crawled slowly up to the station. The conductor and engineer came into the office and expressed their views on being stopped for no apparent reason. My father insisted the signal was clear, and accompanied the crew outside to prove his point.

But the signal arm was straight out — the light was red. He glanced around for an explanation and saw the curly-tailed end of a pig disappearing around the corner of the station-house. My father said to the conductor, "Maybe the pig did it." Snorting in disgust, the conductor high-balled his train and spread the word along the line that the agent at Lorneville had lost his marbles.

A week later my father called me to the station window to bear witness with him. Over in the wye his potatoes had been harvested, but many little ones had been cast aside. The family pig was rooting them out and gorging himself. When he completed his meal he crossed the tracks and trotted along the platform, headed for home.

But for a moment he deviated. He moved inquisitively to the signal lever and drum, thrust his snout into the blob of axle grease on the release cog, then scuttled for his pen and safety behind the house as the drum spun, the cable ran out with a clatter, and the signal jolted from "Go" to "Stop.""

In its day, Lorneville was typical of many diamond junctions where railways of bygone eras intersected. In North America, the 90 degree crossing is a common formation as opposed to Western Europe where railways usually fanned out like spokes of a wheel and where railway engineers tended to avoid this track formation at all costs with its obvious hazards to trains operating at high speed. Even in North America most of these railway intersections had huge signal towers in their heyday, but in the case of Lorneville, the station at the diamond and the four signal arms set out a quarter of a mile away in each direction were considered sufficient to handle the traffic and in hindsight this must have served this junction well, since there is no record of a collision or loss of life at this location throughout its 95 year existence.

Softly now the wind whistles over the silent embankments around this improbable spot in the countryside where if you have a powerful imagination and you concentrate very hard, you may perhaps still hear the distant chant of the stack of an approaching engine and the long ghostly wail of its whistle.

CN 5303 eastbound with train 96 two miles west of Goodwood sometime in 1957/58. This shot illustrates most eloquently the rollicking narrow-gauge road bed. R.J. Sandusky

CN 6167 with a spectacular plume hauling an UCRS excursion into Goodwood, Sunday, January 28, 1962. J. William Hood

A simply delightful scene of GTR #401 on Train 22 at about 9:30 one morning around 1908, about to leave for Uxbridge. Note the Goodwood elevator in excellent trim and the cattle guard in the foreground. Charles H. Heels and PAC C24475

A typical late afternoon scene at Goodwood looking south with the day's quota of milk probably waiting for the Toronto mixed at 3:40 p.m. Mrs. Eleanor Todd

Goodwood's pioneer station became a flagstop in 1951, closed in 1959 and was torn down a year later. Mrs. Eleanor Todd

The exact date and location of this picture are unknown, but according to the owner of this picture, Mr. Tom Nottingham, "Uncle George" and "Uncle Tom" both worked on the T&N out of Uxbridge in the pioneer days and the children on the tender were William, Fred and Eddie Nottingham. The engine is a wood burner with a diamond stack and the link and pin coupler on the tender. The outline of the engine is exactly similar to a Grand Trunk series of 4-4-0s built at the Rhode Island Locomotive Works in Providence, R.I. in 1872. This locomotive could have been assigned to the Midland Railway and if it was assigned to Uxbridge, it would date this picture as being somewhere between 1881 and 1893, since it is unlikely that the GTR would have permitted an engine to operate without road name or number for any length of time. Tom Nottingham and Mrs. Eleanor Todd

An early picture reputedly taken in the Uxbridge area. There are a lot of stumps about, so this could well have been on "the stump dodging line". The engine is GTR 171 built by the Rhode Island Locomotive Works in 1872. It is believed to have been a Midland Railway engine and the number dates the picture as having been taken sometime between 1893 and 1905. Uxbridge-Scott Museum

Platform view of the new GT "witch's hat" station shortly after construction in 1904. The old T&N station is visible in the background. Ontario Archives S15367

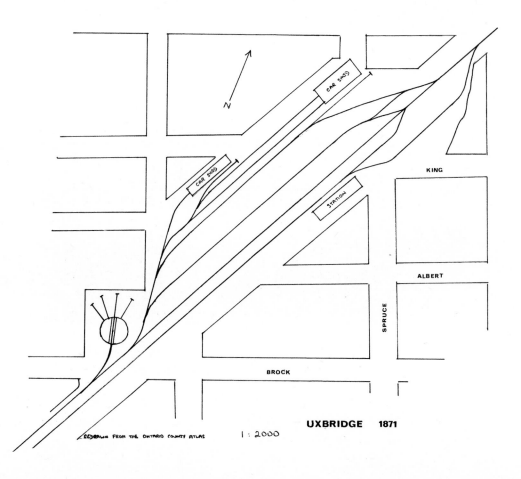

REDRAWN FROM THE ONTARIO COUNTY ATLAS   1 : 2000

UXBRIDGE   1871

KING

ALBERT

SPRUCE

BROCK

CAR SHED

CAR SHED

STATION

Wreck at the north "throat" of the Uxbridge yards. September 24, 1903. PAC PA 47910

GRAND TRUNK 7347

Southbound #92 in charge of CN 5292 ready to go at Uxbridge, February 21, 1959. The Paterson-George Collection

Diesels were appearing on train #96 as shown here with 4403, a three year old GP-9. August 16, 1958. R.J. Sandusky

Uxbridge — A portrait picture taken July 21, 1968. James A. Brown

A rare view of Blackwater Junction basking in the summer sunshine in July 1926. Note the original silhouette of the station including the restaurant in the background. **Murray Spalding**

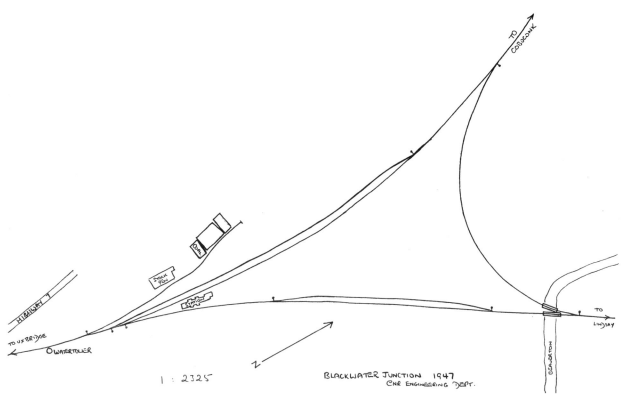

117

Blackwater Junction station on the Lindsay side. 4 January, 1958. R.J. Sandusky

603 leaves Blackwater Junction for Midland, 4 January 1958. The train consists of diesel SP electric motor car 15832 and passenger RPO trailer 15767. R.J. Sandusky

CN 5257 on train 93 (southbound) leaving Blackwater Junction. July 17, 1958. John Rehor

Sunderland in its heyday. It is not clear whether that dandy group of bowlers, fedoras and trilbies is waiting for a train or getting together for a party, but either way let's hope the flat cars get clear of the mainline. Note the freightshed in the background to the right, a view of this T&N model is rare indeed. Ross Thompson

Sunderland looking north in 1969, decidedly vandalized and ready for demolition. James A. Brown

Cannington Station. It burned to the ground in 1968, just three years short of its centenary. Corporation of the Village of Cannington and Gavin Brandon

Joseph Merrifield, station agent at Cannington and grandfather of the owner of this picture, on the job in the early 1920s. Note the morse telegraph key in the window behind him. Art Merrifield

Woodville in the early Grand Trunk days. **Mrs. James Campbell**

A classic portrait of a country railway station taken shortly before demolition in 1966. James A. Brown

The earliest known surviving picture of Lorneville Junction. According to Mr. Heels, this is train number 4 arriving from Midland and due to back out of the station and carry on to Blackwater Junction over the west leg of the wye. Behind the coaches is one of the two old Lorneville hotels which later became a house. To the right of the station is the station agent's house. The Coboconk line would cross approximately where the tender of the locomotive is. Charles H. Heels

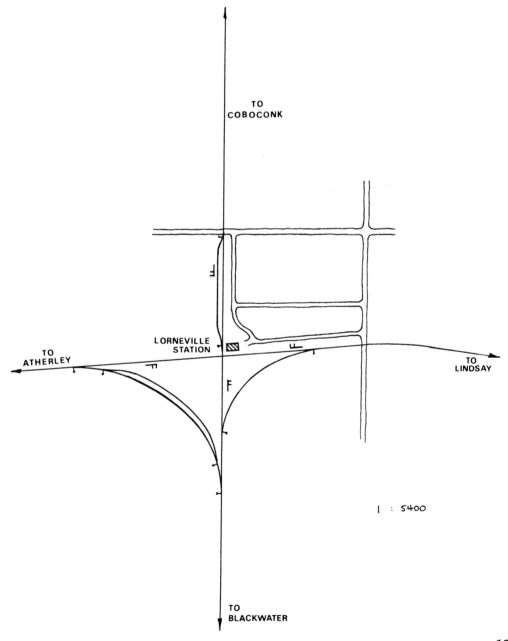

125

The last call for Midland. 603 ready to leave on October 25, 1958. R. J. Sandusky

CN 91 on a work train arrives at Lorneville on its way back to Lindsay, April 25, 1959. CN 91 was the last steam engine to work out of Lindsay and this was her last trip. (The locomotive was subsequently sold and has now been preserved in the U.S.A.) This run ended the steam era "on the Midland" except for subsequent excursions headed by the well-known stars 6167, 6218 and 6060. Hubert Brooks

Out To Coboconk

The Nipissing Guide and Holiday Companion, put out by the T&N as a tourist brochure, tersely summarizes Argyle, Eldon, Portage Road, Kirkfield and Victoria Road as being "all thriving villages giving unlimited supplies of the finest lumber." The railway is now traversing through land that has been obviously more or less cleared of its lumber that must have nigh broken the hearts and determination of the pioneers who came to these parts. Of the villages named, Argyle is next and remains as a pleasant crossroads community. The few buildings left at Eldon, though inhabited, are in an advanced stage of dilapidation bordering on ghost village appearance and Portage Road has disappeared altogether as a recognizable entity. In 1911-12, the Georgian Bay and Seaboard Railway (CPR) came to intersect what was then the GTR in a field just north of the Palestine Quarter Road, and the outline of the right of way is more or less traceable all the way to Kirkfield. The T&N Argyle station sat by the Argyle Quarter Road until its demolition around 1954, the T&N Eldon Station at the Eldon Station Quarter Road surviving until about 1962. The Portage Road Station, of similar design to Eldon, vanished some time earlier around the end of WWII and the slight divergence northwards of Highway 46 gives the station site an appearance of having been much further south of the road than it really was originally. The station access road is still barely traceable today. From its point of intersection with the highway, the line swung east towards Kirkfield, the right of way still identifiable today by a series of utility poles.

The pretty village of Kirkfield was first settled in 1836 and followed the usual pattern of gradual prosperity until the advent of the railway and the decision of the MacKenzie family of Canadian Northern Railway fame to make this village their home away from home. At first the MacKenzies were grain buyers and dealers in the many and varied wood products required by the railway contractors, especially poles, posts and ties. There were also grist and woollen mills but by 1890 the boom had started to level off. It is now a village of new homes and summer retreats with a rapidly dwindling number of residents who can still trace their pioneer residence back to the last century. Among boating enthusiasts, Kirkfield is best known for its lift lock and among railway buffs for the stone quarry which used to be reached by taking the back road round by the lock, unless of course one walked in by the railway line itself, a route no longer possible with the removal of the railway bridge across the Trent-Severn water channel.

The stone quarry had a double attraction in its heyday because its countless shipments of stone provided some spectacular sights of heavy motive power, sometimes double-headed, pounding along the right of way to Toronto, Lindsay or even Atherley on occasion (and thus keeping the Coboconk subdivision going for many a year when it might well otherwise have been torn out in the Depression). But the quarry itself had a fascinating internal 3' narrow gauge operation for hauling the stone from the rock face to the gigantic crusher which dominated the landscape. The operation was originally started up around 1907-08, crushing first of all the left-over stone from the building of the Trent-Severn Canal. It eventually became a village of its own with around 30 company houses when the owner, by the name of George Essery, started his own quarrying operation with a larger crusher at which time the railway facilities were enlarged. The quarry's capacity in its best years was around 25-30 gondola cars daily of crushed stone and there was at least one train a day out of the quarry at the peak of its production years. Sadly, the quarry ceased operations in 1961 and the fate of the Coboconk subdivision was sealed.

Once past the quarry, the next settlement to be served, with a station very similar in design to Kirkfield's, was Victoria Road, a village that also grew up with the railway. Situated on Highway 505 at the northerly tip of Mitchell Lake, Victoria Road once boasted a saw mill and the usual variety of village businesses including "the world's largest general store," closed up now for some 25 years, although the building still stands to the left as one enters the village from the south. At the station, there was a loop siding and Mr. Esler Smith, our informative section foreman for many years on the Midland subdivision, recalls being told that in the early days there was a spur line into a gravel pit just south of the main railway line.

Right after Victoria Road, there was another fascinating early industrial venture as the line passed picturesque Raven Lake. This was the Raven Lake Portland Cement Company's plant and this condensed account from "The Land Between" by F.V. LeCraw gives us the details:

"The Company proposed to build a cement plant between the GTR track and the south shore of Raven Lake. Power to run the plant was to be generated at Elliott's Falls, about 13 miles from Raven Lake. Work began on the powerhouse in 1903. Meanwhile, at Raven Lake, a huge plant of stone and cement was being constructed. It was to be a six kiln plant of the most modern design, representing the latest ideas in the economic manufacture of cement. Scheduled to start operating in 1904, the plant had an output of 700 barrels of cement every 24 hours. The raw material came from the bottom of Raven Lake which was covered with a deposit of marl ten to twenty feet deep. Clay came in from Beaverton on flat cars and was dried, ground and stored in overhead bins. The kilns were coal fired, the coal coming in by train. All the machinery was powered by electric motors. At the peak of operation, some 200 men were employed on the site. The Company's product was of good quality and was named, appropriately, 'Raven' Brand Cement. The Company ceased operations in 1914, a victim of the Free Trade Agreement with the United States allowing cement to come into Canada at a price so low that Raven Lake could not compete. The plant machinery was sold to the Canada Cement Company and the steel beams supporting the roof went to the Town of Haliburton for a new ice hockey arena."

The ruins are still hidden away on private property beside the lake and the spur line right of way is clearly visible. Mr. Esler Smith remembers being in charge of lifting the rails of the Raven Lake Siding in 1927, at which time he recalls, the old style stub switches east of Kirkfield were finally replaced by the conventional type blade switches.

After Raven Lake the line passed through Corson's Siding, an historically named flagstop and community. Mrs. Grace Peel, a lifelong friend of the Corson family, recalls that the community was named after Captain John Corson, a lake captain, who came to Corson's to manage the Gooderham & Worts timber limit adjacent to the siding. He also looked after a local G&W lime kiln operation which supplied the Toronto Gas Works with the lime necessary for the manufacture of carbide gas before the days of electricity. Captain Corson acquired his own property in the area including charcoal and sawmill operations, both of which were lost in a large fire which swept through the area in the late 1800s, after which the Corson family went into the lime business themselves. Captain Corson died in 1908 and the need for lime gradually decreased until this last local enterprise faded away altogether. Today Corson's Siding is a peaceful little hamlet and it would take a sharp eye to locate the road bed.

Our Nipissing Holiday Companion now brings us to the end of the journey:

"Two miles further on, we come to the North Bay Bridge, a very high structure over an arm of Balsam Lake. As the train is moved across the bridge, we obtain a view of one of the most lovely landscapes of original Canadian scenery. Gradually unfolded before us is a panorama of the country bordering on Balsam Lake and which, whether seen in the glaring light of the mid-day sun, or in the soft reflected rays of a cloudless sunset; whether viewed in the deep, rich, vernal colour, or in the varied and gorgeous tints of the incomparable Canadian autumn; is a picture of marvellous natural beauty, to which even the inspired hand of an Angelo, or the magic brush of a Raphael, would fail to render justice upon canvas."

If one may suspect that the writer of this brochure was none other than George Laidlaw himself in view of the fact that we know he was the author of so much written eloquence, one may be left with the feeling that he was describing his own homestead; that he had come home and that he knew whereof he wrote.

Before the coming of the railway, Coboconk was a dot on the map but its history and development are also linked with the steamboats and all the pine that could come south by land and water. It was here that the "Shedden House" was built, the companion structure to the Laidlaw House at Cannington, and in a flush of enthusiasm the community was actually called Shedden between 1873 and 1880. In this heyday, the village boasted a large steam sawmill, three hotels, several stores and a population of over 400. The steamer "Coboconk" (1875-1887) plied between Fenelon Falls and Coboconk, linking the Victoria Railway with the T&N through the rebuilt Rosedale lock. In those days, millions of square feet of timber left Coboconk, situated on the Gull River just above where it empties into Balsam Lake, and this commerce was crucial to the development of the Haliburton Highlands. The coming of the railway also attracted many visitors and holiday makers to an unspoiled corner of Ontario. It was abundant with scenery, game fish and fresh air; and once out of earshot of the scream of the sawmill, with peace and tranquility; broken only by the occasional distant throaty steamboat whistle.

Today, the Village of Coboconk gets along without its railway as best as it can. In its mature years, Highway 35 affords a direct link with Lindsay with which the railway could not compete anyway as far as passenger traffic was concerned, but the tourists and the cottage owners still come to "Coby" to do their shopping or to pause on their journey.

Of the railway itself, little trace remains as the yard and station area has been taken over by local businesses. The station itself has survived as a captive structure and as one looks back through the chain link fence towards the west, one can see a foot path receding into the hillocks that was once the right of way.

It is the sad end of an unfinished dream.

The Argyle flag-station in the tidy Grand Trunk days. The local grain shed is to the left (north) of the station building. The station was razed in 1954. **Mr. and Mrs. Frank Sweet**

Double-header stone train (Mikados 3228 and 3272) high-balling past Argyle on August 8, 1958. (This same train was also photographed at Woodville and Blackwater Junction.) John Rehor

Signal tower at Argyle where the Georgian Bay and Seaboard Railway crossed the Grand Trunk in an open field. Demolished with the abandonment of the GB&S in 1937. Victor Dunn

Jim and Bill Gordon on the jigger at Eldon. ca 1920. Victor Dunn

A folding picture postcard view of Eldon station taken around the turn of the century. The grain house is in the distance. The view is looking south. Mrs. William McFadden

A family outing, believed to be at the Portage Road Station. Victor Dunn

The Coboconk mixed at Kirkfield Station in September, 1951. Looking west. R.J. Sandusky

Kirkfield Station just after the weeds took over and the chimbley came a-tumbling down. Fortunately this building was sold and is being preserved on location. It is an original T&N building similar in design to Victoria Road and the (first) Coboconk Station. James A. Brown

CN 2516 pauses with its mixed train from Coboconk to pick up some stone laden gondolas at the quarry. September 1951. R.J. Sandusky

CN 2516 has paused to pick up some laden gondolas at the quarry and is now approaching the Trent Canal. September, 1951. R.J. Sandusky

A narrow gauge train in the Kirkfield quarry about 1930. Ken Wilson

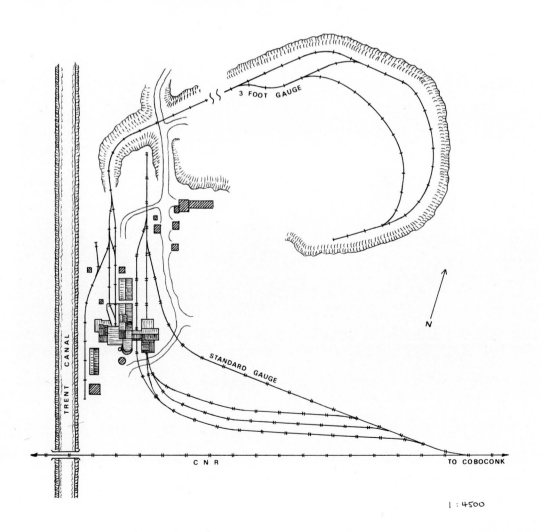

3 FOOT GAUGE

N

STANDARD GAUGE

TRENT CANAL

C N R

TO COBOCONK

1 : 4500

A general view of the quarry and the narrow gauge system. As usual, there are two locomotives "in steam". The train on the left is coasting down to the loading area and on the right is a loaded train beginning its arduous ascent to the crusher. September, 1954. R.J. Sandusky

A view of the 3' gauge yard from the unloading ramp. The entire roster of 0-4-0s is in sight (2 active and 1 spare). On the left is the spur to the machine shop alongside the Trent Canal. Beyond the locomotives the track curves to the right into the quarry. September 1959. R.J. Sandusky

Kirkfield Crushed Stone's standard gauge 0-4-0, in the usual unlettered, unnumbered state which was common for many such machines. It was built by the Montreal Locomotive Works (#54319) and following abandonment of the quarry, was stored at Atherley for a number of years and is now displayed at the Simcoe County Museum at Midhurst, Ontario. 19 June 1939. J.D. Knowles

The narrow gauge engines working their hearts (tubes?) out in the quarry, near the end. 1960 R.F. Corley

The Vulcan narrow gauge engine on the spare track. 1960 R.F. Corley

The quarry has closed and this narrow gauge locomotive has been sold off. For the men who worked with these engines for years it must have been a sad occasion to see their old friends being shipped off to destinations unknown. Ken Wilson

Victoria Road Station looking towards Coboconk. ca 1910 Wilf Anthony, Toronto Postcard Club

CN 2516 arrives at Victoria Road enroute to Coboconk in September, 1951. Scarcely a mixed train here; these were memorable trips for the passengers when a cattle car was cut in ahead of the coach, an old-timer with its arch windows still intact. R.J. Sandusky

The "Coby" mixed pulling out of Victoria Road on its way to Lindsay one fine day in September, 1951. R.J. Sandusky

When this picture was taken, this view was not a big deal. Today it is an irreplaceable souvenir of a branch line right of way. Somewhere between Victoria Road and Coby in June 1950. R.J. Sandusky

The top of the North Bay trestle looking towards Coby in September, 1951. R.J. Sandusky

A rare picture of the Coby mixed about to master the last gradient before its destination as it crosses the North Bay trestle some time in the early 1950s. Burrell Stevens

Daddy was not on the engine, but a kindly hogger would occasionally give a kid a joyride into Coby and thus the precious memory of a lifetime. Burrell Stevens

"1908. August 4th. A dreadful thunderstorm last night. The railway station burnt to the ground with the lightning". Ruth Sangster diary

A westbound view from the road around the turn of the century with an exceptionally detailed outline of the original T&N station building. W.J. Peel

A quick game of tennis before train time. A view from the leisurely years with the original station building as back drop. Probably ca 1905 as this station was struck by lightning and burnt to the ground in August 1908.
F.V. LeCraw

The Coboconk station jigger outside its shed at the west end of the yard. Left is Jack Coates, section foreman, and to the right Jack Liscombe, section man. Note the three way turnout on the approach to Coby. Miss W. Liscombe

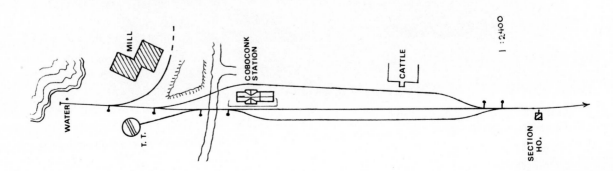

Very early view of what appears to be an outing ready to leave Coby. Probably ca 1890. N. Ryckman

A delightful view of the station and the "Coby Express" on August 27,1941, when Highway 35 was still a dirt track and if you wanted to conserve your gas coupons, the train was the way to go. Lloyd Baxter

November 23, 1957. R.J. Sandusky

2516 sits at the very end track past where the water tower used to be, now taking on water from a standpipe. The water is being syphoned up from the lake by steam, almost Haggas elevator style. September, 1951. R.J. Sandusky

Turntable lead to the left, mill spur to the right. September, 1951. R.J. Sandusky

CN 2516 just turned on the Coby table. September 1951 R.J. Sandusky

Consolidation-type 2644 switching at the west end of the Coboconk yard. She is rearranging some freight cars as the passenger excursion train has crowded the capacity of the yard somewhat. 29 September, 1956. R.J. Sandusky

Coboconk from the cab roof of 5592 on the terminal stub. The turntable is to the right. 17 June, 1950 R.J. Sandusky

146

Taking a good look around while they may. UCRS excursion. 17 June 1950. Hubert Brooks

The UCRS 1950 excursion. Hubert Brooks

A crowd of admirers watching 5592 being turned.
17 June, 1950 Hubert Brooks

His last chance. Hubert Brooks

July 16, 1965. W.J. Dickinson

149

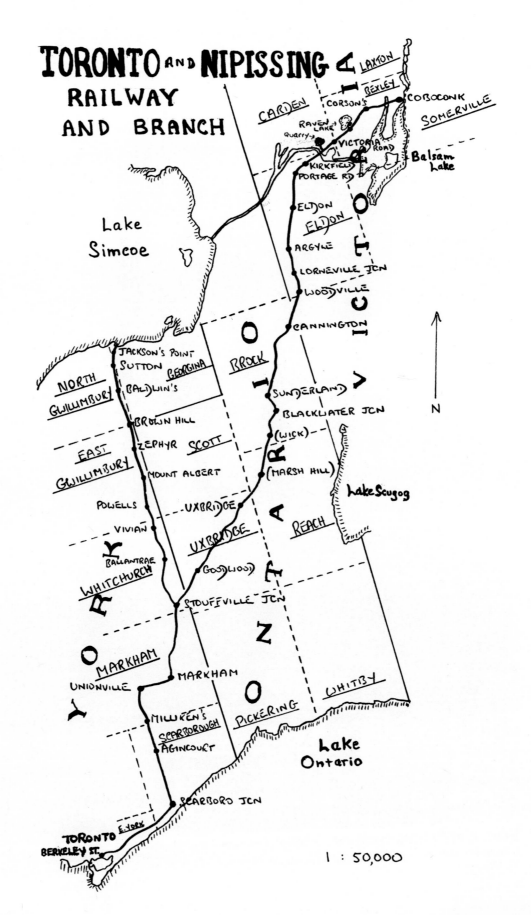

TORONTO AND NIPISSING
RAILWAY
AND BRANCH

1 : 50,000

150

Epilogue

The irony of it all is that the justification for this railway today is as valid as it was a century ago. If cordwood was the energy worry of the 1870s, oil is certainly the energy problem of the 1980s. As this book was being written, three things of significance happened. Firstly, in an incredibly short-sighted move, the rails into Sutton were ripped out. Secondly, the daily Stouffville commuter service was actually threatened with cancellation. This was followed within just a matter of weeks with the certainty of an energy program which will more than double the cost of gasoline at today's prices within a scant few years. In fact, the automobile as we know it and use it today is doomed. Just as the public of 100 years ago was often misled about the benefits that would accrue if this or that railway were built, this same public is now being blandished to believe that their future is in Pickering airports and superhighways. In fact, their future is right on the ground, right on those rusty rails held together by those rotting ties where their dilapidated station used to be 20 years ago. Let us hope that the good people of Brock and people everywhere rise again to stop this insanity of abandonment.

Last, but not least, there is this to consider. Those who have argued that the public has a right to railway service as a matter of heritage have been belittled as also arguing for the return of steam boats, velocipedes, and stage coaches. However, that put-down ignores two things:

Railways in modern technology are still the most efficient means of moving people and cargo. Secondly, our railways were paid for by the public purse in the first place; in fact somewhere in the gross national debt we are still paying for them (undoubtedly also for the Toronto and Nipissing Railway) and the public is entitled to retain for the public good what has been dearly paid for by every Canadian, living and dead, for the past 100 years, not just in hard-earned cash; but by many of them also in blood, sweat, toil and tears.

It is something to think about.

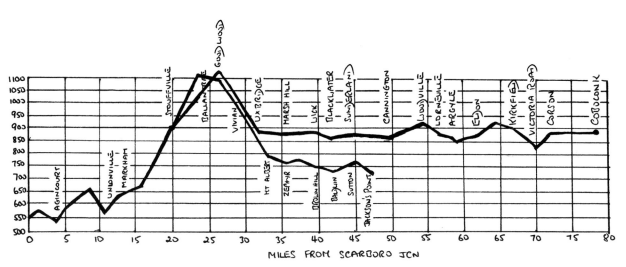

REDRAWN FROM AN ORIGINAL BY DE ROSS.

Chronology

26 Dec. 1846   Peterborough and Port Hope Rly chartered.

16 May 1853   First train of the Ontario, Simcoe & Huron Union RR to Machell's Corners (Aurora).

27 Oct. 1856   First through GTR service between Montreal and Toronto.

16 Oct. 1857   PH, L&B arrives in Lindsay.

Early 1857   GTR connects Don Station and Queen's Wharf termini.

Apr. 1858   Gooderham & Worts distillery building opened.

May 1858   First Union Station, Toronto.

4 Mar. 1868   T&N and T, G&B charters passed.

23 Jan. 1869   T&N charter amended to construct branch to Lindsay.

16 Oct. 1869   T&N Sodturning Ceremony at Cannington.

1869   Edmund Wragge arrives in Toronto to take up his combined appointment as Chief Engineer of the T, G&B and the T&N Railways.

Mar. 1870   John Shedden takes over as President of the T&N

1 Jan. 1871   PH, L&B (now the Midland Railway) arrives in Beaverton.

23 May 1871   First T&N passenger train to Uxbridge.

12 July 1871   T&N opens for traffic to Uxbridge.

14 Sept. 1871   Grand opening ceremony of the T&N, Uxbridge.

Oct. 1871   T&N reaches Cannington.

Mar. 1872   Preliminary discussion re Lake Simcoe Junction Railway (LSJR) takes place.

1872   T&N Wharf at Berkeley Street opens.

26 Nov. 1872   T&N opens to Coboconk.

29 Mar. 1873   LSJR charter passed.

Spring 1873   The "Shedden" is delivered to the T&N.

16 May 1873   John Shedden killed at Cannington Station.

22 July 1873   PH, L&B (now the Midland Rly) arrives in Orillia.

31 Jan. 1874   The "Shedden" explodes at Stouffville.

June 1874   Midland Rly of Canada converts from 5'6" to 4'8½" gauge.

4 Sept. 1875   Edmund Wragge becomes General Manager of the T, G&B. J.C. Bailey becomes Chief Engineer of the T&N.

10 Feb. 1876   LSJR charter amended to extend to the Whitby and Port Perry Rly.

19 Oct. 1876   LSJR agreement with T&N ratified.

1 Oct. 1877   LSJR opens for traffic.

1879   "Large wharf" at Jackson's Point completed.

July 1881   The T&N bought out by Midland Railway.

12 Dec. 1881   "Midland Consolidation" (of the T&N and other railways) ratified.

15 Dec. 1881   First through train Peterborough to Toronto via Lorneville Junction on the 4'8½' gauge.

10 Mar. 1882   "Midland Consolidation" becomes law (45 VIC Cap 67).

1 Apr. 1882   "Midland Consolidation" becomes effective.

Summer 1883   Manilla Junction to Wick Junction (T&O charter) opened to traffic and third rail lifted from Lorneville to Toronto.

15 Aug. 1883   Lorneville to Coboconk section converted to 4'8½".

26 Oct. 1883   LSJR converted to 4'8½".

1 Jan. 1884   Omemee to Peterborough "Missing Link" (T&O charter) opened.

1 Jan. 1884   Consolidated Midland Rly leased to GTR.

6 Aug. 1889   George Laidlaw dies at Balsam Lake.

25 Oct.1892   Consolidation of the Midland Railway and LSJR into GTR ratified.

1 Apr. 1893   Consolidation of Midland Railway and LSJR into GTR becomes effective.

1907/8   Kirkfield Quarry opens.

24 Sept. 1927   Line closed from Sutton to Jackson's Point.

25 Sept. 1927   Abandonment of "the Old Road" (Millbrook Jen to Omemee).

19 May 1928   Mixed train service discontinued on the Sutton Branch.

12-25 Oct. 1928   Rails lifted between Ballantrae and Zephyr.

1930   Spur lifted between Stouffville and Ballantrae.

25 Mar. 1955   Mixed train service ceases to Coboconk.

25 Apr. 1959   Last steam locomotive in regular service on the Midland Subdivision.

1961   Kirkfield Quarry closes.

31 Jan.1962   Last Belleville-Toronto passenger train, ending all passenger service on the old Midland system except for the newly instituted Toronto-Markham commuter service (evening only).

30 Mar. 1965   Last freight service to Coboconk.

16 July 1965   Rails lifted on Coboconk section.

31 July 1966   Woodville to Lorneville Junction and Lindsay to Beaverton sections abandoned (rails lifted 1967).

28 June 1971   Stouffville commuter service (a.m. & p.m.) ordered by the CTC, replacing the Toronto-Markham service.

13 Aug. 1979   Sutton Branch switch "spiked" at Zephyr.

14 July 1981   Rails lifted on the remainder of the Sutton Branch.

7 Sept. 1982   First GO-train slated to take over from the VIA passenger service to Stouffville.

THE TORONTO & NIPISSING RLY AND BRANCH

IN THE MIDLAND SYSTEM 1882-93

Senator George Albertus Cox — 1840-1914. Life insurance agent, politician and financier. Vice-President of the Midland Railway of Canada at the time of lease to the GTR. The Canada Life Assurance Company

N ←

HALIBURTON

KINMOUNT

COBOCONK

FENELON FALLS

VICTORIA ROAD

KIRKFIELD

PORTAGE ROAD

COCO ISLAND SIDING

ELDON

ARGYLE

LORNEVILLE JCN

WOODVILLE

CANNINGTON

SUNDERLAND

MANILLA JCN

BLACKWATER JCN

(WICK)

(MARSH HILL)

PORT PERRY

UXBRIDGE

GOODWOOD

LINDSAY

OMEMEE

LAKEFIELD

PETERBOROUGH

MILLBROOK JCN

PORT HOPE

ELDORADO

MADOC

MADOC JCN

ROSLIN?

BELLEVILLE

ORILLIA

LAKE SIMCOE

BEAVERTON

JACKSON'S POINT

SUTTON

BALDWIN'S

BROWN HILL

ZEPHYR

MOUNT ALBERT

POLELLS

VIVIAN

BALLANTRAE

STOUFFVILLE JCN

MARKHAM

UNIONVILLE

MILLIKEN'S

AGINCOURT

SCARBORO JCN

G.T.R.

DON NORTH (LATER)

QUEEN PAGE (LATER)

BERKELEY STREET

MIDLAND

WHITBY

LAKE ONTARIO

1 : 72,500

Special Acknowledgements

To the helpful staff at:

    The Public Archives of Canada
    The CN Archives
    The Archives of Ontario
    The Metropolitan Toronto Library Board (including the Canadiana Collection, Fairview Mall Library)
    The City Hall Archives, Toronto
    The Markham District Historical Museum
    The Uxbridge-Scott Museum
    The Whitchurch-Stouffville Museum
    The Georgina Village Museum
    The Cannington Museum
    The Cannington Municipal Office
    The Victoria Museum
    The Mackenzie House, Kirkfield

and the Public Libraries at Mount Albert, Sunderland, Cannington and Woodville.

To Mrs. Jean Shields, granddaughter of George Laidlaw, who coordinated and made available to me much local history in the Coboconk area, as well as family history pertaining to her grandfather and also lent to me or borrowed on my behalf many pictures from several generous local residents; thereby saving me much precious time.

To Mr. Charles Heels, veteran railroad historian at Lindsay, who contributed several pictures, much time and many precious recollections.

To Mr. John Lunau, Curator of the Markham District Historical Museum, who opened up the museum picture collection to me and also made available the museum copy of the microfilmed Markham Economist (now the Markham Economist & Sun).

To Mr. George Horner, a veteran CNR railroader who has generously contributed much historical and operational data, including timetable information.

To Mr. Hubert Brooks, who painted and contributed the watercolour which is featured on the dust jacket of this book.

To my mother, Mrs. Ruth Cooper, who wrote countless letters and made visits to the Leeds (Yorkshire) Public Library and the Hunslet Locomotive Works in pursuit of the history of the Fairlie Locomotive.

To all those who allowed their pictures to be copied and used in this book, but in particular to Messrs R.J. (Bob) Sandusky, James A. Brown, J. William Hood, John Rehor and the Paterson-George Collection, whose professional pictures made a vital contribution to the "latter-day" scene portrayed in this book.

To the Toronto Postcard Club who searched on my behalf for early scenes, and to Mr. Wilf Anthony in particular who allowed a number of precious cards from his collection to be reproduced.

To Mr. Ray Corley, an acknowledged expert on the history of the Midland Railway, for reviewing the manuscript and making a number of helpful suggestions and corrections.

To the many others who have provided assistance, information, clues, leads, checked references, and in some cases loaned material; with a request by the author for indulgence by anyone who has not been named since the contributors are many indeed:

Mr. Herbert Bartholomew
Mr. and Mrs. William Chapelle, Sutton
Mr. Tom Dickson
Mrs. John Eakins
Mr. Ross P. Ellerbeck, Uxbridge
Mr. Edward Emery
Mr. A. Fraser Fairlie, CN Public Affairs, Toronto
The Festiniog Railway Company, Wales
Mr. Rae Fleming, Argyle
Mr. Stephen Gooderham
Mrs. Sarah Hancock, Woodville
Mr. Ivan Harris, Stouffville
Mr. Dinty Hodgins, Stouffville
Mr. Elmer Jordan, Lorneville
Mrs. Orland Lamb, Woodville
Mr. W. Latimer, Markham
Mr. Eugene Lemon, Bloomington
Mrs. Nena Marsden, Sutton
Mrs. William McFadden
Mr. Art Merrifield
Mr. George Mitchell
Mr. Tom Nottingham
Mrs. Pat Phillips, Unionville
Mrs. Margaret Rose
Mrs. Zelda Rose, Brown Hill
Mrs. Gladys Rolling, Mount Albert
Mrs. D. St. John, Uxbridge
Mr. Harold Sanders, QC, Jackson's Point
Mr. Reeford Sedore, Brown Hill
Mr. William Sellers, Sutton
Mr. Esler Smith
Mr. Dave Spaulding
Mr. Burrell Stevens
Mr. Ross Thompson, Sunderland
Mr. J.E. Tisdale, Q.C., Simcoe
Mrs. Eleanor Todd, Goodwood
Mr. Herb Wilson, Kirkfield

To Mr. Ralph Beaumont and The Boston Mills Press for being an enthusiastic and empathetic publisher.

To Mrs. Marilyn Findlay and Mrs. Valerie Jordan for having the patience to type the copy.

To my family for their support and encouragement during the hours of travail.

Bibliography

G.R. Stevens
Canadian National Railways (Sixty Years of Trial and Error) Vol. 1. Clarke, Irwin & Company Limited, 1960.

Robert Dorman
A Statutory History of the Steam and Electric Railways of Canada 1836-1937. Queen's Printer, Ottawa.

James White
Altitudes in Canada. Commission of Conservation Canada 1915.

Myles Pennington, 1814-1898
Railways and Other Ways, Being Reminiscences of Canal and Railway Life over 67 Years.

Ontario and Dominion Statutes
(courtesy Weir & Foulds Legal Library, Barristers and Solicitors, Toronto)

County Atlases
York, Ontario, Atlas of the Dominion of Canada (Victoria County)

E.B. Shuttleworth
The Windmill and its Times. 1924

Richard Tatley
Steamboating on the Trent-Severn. MIKA Publishing Company, Belleville, 1978.

Omer Lavallée
Narrow Gauge Railways of Canada. Railfare Enterprises Ltd. 1972.

Leo A. Johnson
History of the County of Ontario 1615-1875. The Corporation of the County of Ontario.

J.M. and Edward Trout
The Railways of Canada. 1871

L.T.C. Rolt
Red for Danger. The Bodley Head. 1955

Charles H. Heels
Railroad Recollections. Museum Restoration Service. 1980

Rowland A.S. Abbott
The Fairlie Locomotive. David and Charles. 1970

A Traveller's Guide to the Festiniog Railway.
Festiniog Railway Company

Narrow Gauge Railways of Wales.
   Jarrold and Sons Ltd. 1973

A Guide to the Great Little Trains of Wales.

Nick and Helma Mika
   Railways of Canada. McGraw-Hill Ryerson Limited. 1978

James Filby
   Credit Valley Railway. Boston Mills Press. 1974

R.F. Corley
   Preserved Canadian Railway Equipment. Railfare Enterprises Limited. 1972

T.F. McIlwraith, Jr.
   The Toronto Grey and Bruce Railway. UCRS Bulletin 56. 1963

Early British Railways
   King Penguin

The Concise Dictionary of National Biography
   Oxford University Press

L.T.C. Rolt
   A Hunslet 100. David and Charles. 1964

G.P. de T. Glazebrook
   The Story of Toronto. University of Toronto Press. 1971

D.C. Masters
   The Rise of Toronto 1850-1890. University of Toronto Press. 1947

C. Pelham Mulvany
   Toronto: Past and Present. W.E. Caiger. 1884

Markham 1793-1900
   Edited by Isabel Champion. Published by the Markham Historical Society. 1979

Stouffville: A Pictorial History: 1877-1977
   Compiled by Jean Barkey. Published by the Stouffville Historical Committee

Peterborough — Land of Shining Waters — An Anthology
   A Centennial Volume published by the City and County of Peterborough. University
   of Toronto Press 1967. (Iron Roads — R.F. Corley)

Mrs. Ross N. Carr
   Land of Plenty. Published by the Ops Township Council. 1968

F.V. LeCraw
    The Land Between. Published by Laxton, Digby and Longford Council. 1967

Mrs. Islay Lambert
    Call Them Blessed. The Corporation of the Village of Cannington. 1971

Mrs. Gladys M. Rolling
    East Gwillimbury in the Nineteenth Century.

Rae Fleming
    Argyle — A Pioneering Village

W.H. Higgins
    The Life and Times of Joseph Gould. Fitzhenry & Whiteside. 1972

Mrs. Eleanor Todd
    Burrs and Blackberries From Goodwood. 1980

A History of Scarborough.
    Edited by Robert R. Bonis and published by the Scarborough Public Library.

Watson Kirkconnell
    County of Victoria Centennial History. Victoria County Council. 1967

Living History of Brock and Scugog Townships

Georgina — History of a Township
    Lake Simcoe South Shore Historical Society

John C. Bailey Papers (Ontario Archives)

F. Shanly Papers (Ontario Archives)

Since 1847 — The Canada Life Story

UCRS Newsletters

CRHA News Reports

1867 — George Laidlaw — Reports and letters on light narrow gauge railways (Ontario Archives)

1867 — Cheap Railways — George Laidlaw — pamphlet (Ontario Archives)

T&N and LSJR Minute Books (Public Archives of Canada)

And miscellaneous references which have been acknowledged in the text.